Trudging the Road

Trudging the Road

A Work/Study
Journey through the Twelve Steps
of Alcoholics Anonymous

By

Chris F. Gladding

Trudging the Road

A Work/Study
Journey through the Twelve Steps
of Alcoholics Anonymous

Published by:
GLAD PUBLICATION
966 Palmwood Drive
Sparks, NV 89434
Tel.: 702 356-7856

ISBN 0-9629091-0-6

Printed in the United States of America

Lindley
Thank You for all your
help and friendship.
God Bless
Chris Gladding
3-19-91

To Kim Gladding, Carl Hebert and Cherie Galbreath;
the embodiment of Love and Friendship.

CONTENTS

LESSONS:

CONTENTS

CONTENTS

CHARTS:

ACKNOWLEDGEMENT

I want to express my gratitude to three special friends, Carl Hebert, Sharyn Peal and Lindley Steere. Without Carl's effort at proofing and editing this work, timely publication would have been impossible. The credit for the title belongs to Carl; he has been a true friend in every sense of the word. The input from Sharyn and Lindley while proofing this work has provided a valuable service for publication. I offer a sincere "Thank You" to the Reno Fire Department, especially the Safety/Training Division, for their assistance and community–minded spirit. Finally, I would like to express my love and affection for God's gifts to me: Kim, a loving and supportive daughter; Verna and Steve, my parents; Gil and Danny, my brothers; Gail, my father; and Lucy, my faithful "assistant." Thank You to Patsy, a very special lady, and her family. Finally, I would never have written this work without God to direct my thoughts and guide my pen. "Thank You" seems so inadequate. . .

INTRODUCTION

This work/study guide is designed to bring to light important principles and concepts in the program of Alcoholics Anonymous. When I prepared it, I was mindful of the need to validate in the text of the books ALCOHOLICS ANONYMOUS and TWELVE STEPS AND TWELVE TRADITIONS the answers to the questions asked. The user will notice the page numbers in parentheses at the end of every question. A plain number in parentheses means the answer can be found on that page in the book ALCOHOLICS ANONYMOUS, Third Edition. For example, a question followed by (58) keys the reader to page 58 in the text. A question bearing the notation (12x12, 48) means that the answer can be located at page 48 in the text of the book TWELVE STEPS AND TWELVE TRADITIONS. The page references are for the later printings of both books. Even though the information is the same in all printings of the book TWELVE STEPS AND TWELVE TRADITIONS, the information in older printings is found on different pages.

There are a limited number of questions which make a statement and ask the user to agree or disagree after reviewing the pages cited in the two texts. Some may feel that these are statements of opinion; acknowledging this possibility, I have made every attempt to thoroughly verify the statements in the two texts. For those who disagree, I would be pleased to receive your criticisms and corrections.

This guide is on the steps of recovery; therefore, I have not asked any questions on the Twelve Traditions. Some questions may be difficult to answer or explain. Consequently. I have included the answers at the back of the guide. The value of this work will come if the user will: **1**. read the chapter or portion of the chapter in both texts which corresponds with each lesson; **2**. answer as many of the questions as possible in a lesson without resort to the texts; **3**. then try to find the correct answers in the texts, and **4**. finally, compare the attempted answers to the answers given at the back of the guide. This process should greatly enhance the user's depth of learning. I believe that simply telling the answer has little value; my intent was to help people understand what the texts demonstrate is the most effective path to recovery. When people help each other find, learn and understand correct A.A. information, each can then make their own value judgment and apply the information to their particular circumstances. An especially useful setting for this learning tool is the **sponsorship relationship**; the guide was **not** designed to replace the person who has experience with the path of recovery.

Incorporation of the principles and concepts of Alcoholics Anonymous into the very fabric of a member's life is essential to resisting the obsession to drink. I firmly believe that as long as sobriety is external, it will not be long before alcohol becomes internal.

In an effort to help others understand the simple path to recovery, I have included an illustration on the next page. It shows the need for a guiding purpose, undergirded by goals and objectives designed to fill those goals. This framework – strong purpose, goals, and objectives (footwork) is necessary to a reasonable and achievable path to recovery. With these ideas firmly imprinted on the mind and the actions which follow as a result, the recovering alcoholic may not sacrifice the long term goal for short term satisfaction. This guide may be classified in the area of footwork or objectives. Hopefully, it will provide some answers about the steps of recovery. I have included a number of other illustrations at the back of the guide to help others understand various concepts and ideas.

INTRODUCTION

An informative adjunct for understanding the A.A. model of recovery are two books by William Glasser, MD. These books are not in any way connected with or about A.A.

The book, CONTROL THEORY, explains why, and to a great extent how, all living organisms behave and that all we do all of our lives is behave. It contends that all of our behavior is purposeful and that purpose is always to attempt to satisfy basic needs that are built into our genetic structure. It is called control theory because all behavior is our best attempt at the time to control ourselves (so that we can control the world we live in) as we continually try to satisfy one or more of these basic needs.

The book, REALITY THERAPY, teaches a method of counseling based on control theory which is aimed at helping counselees to gain more effective control over their own lives. It can also be used by individuals to improve the effectiveness of their own lives. It is an approach that also has been proven effective in education, parenting, leadership and managing or in any situation where people need to learn how to satisfy their needs in responsible ways. It is based on the belief that we all choose what we do with our lives and that we are responsible for these choices. Reality therapy defines responsibility as learning to choose behaviors that satisfy our needs and, at the same time, do not deprive others of a chance to do the same. The key components as used by counselors are to persuade clients to take an honest look at both what they **want** and what they are **doing** to get what they want. Assuming they are frustrated, or are frustrating others, they are taught to evaluate what they are **doing** and, from this evaluation, both learn and put into practice more effective (need-satisfying) **behaviors**.

I highly recommend these books for study. Those interested can become Reality Therapy Certified by the Institute For Reality Therapy, 7301 Medical Center Drive, Suite 202, Canoga Park, California, 91307, telehone 818-888-0688, after a two year course of study.

Some users may wonder about the title to this guide. It seems to imply a plodding, struggling walk through recovery (life). An old understanding for the meaning of the word "trudge" is to walk with dignity in one's circumstances. With that idea in mind, I settled on the title "Trudging the Road: A Work/Study Journey through the Twelve Steps of Alcoholics Anonymous," or walking with dignity in one's circumstances on the road of life.

I hope you will find this guide beneficial in your recovery or in helping someone else. If you are a professional in the field of alcoholism, my aim is to provide you with another resource in your effort to help the suffering alcoholic.

A final note: this work does not reflect the official position of Alcoholics Anonymous, nor is it endorsed by Alcoholics Anonymous. For better or worse, it is a product of my efforts, and I take full responsibility for any errors in doctrine or interpretation. Hopefully, there are few.

Our Purpose shapes our Goals
which in turn, define our Objectives.
When we work on our Objectives
we meet our Goals and thereby fulfill our Purpose.

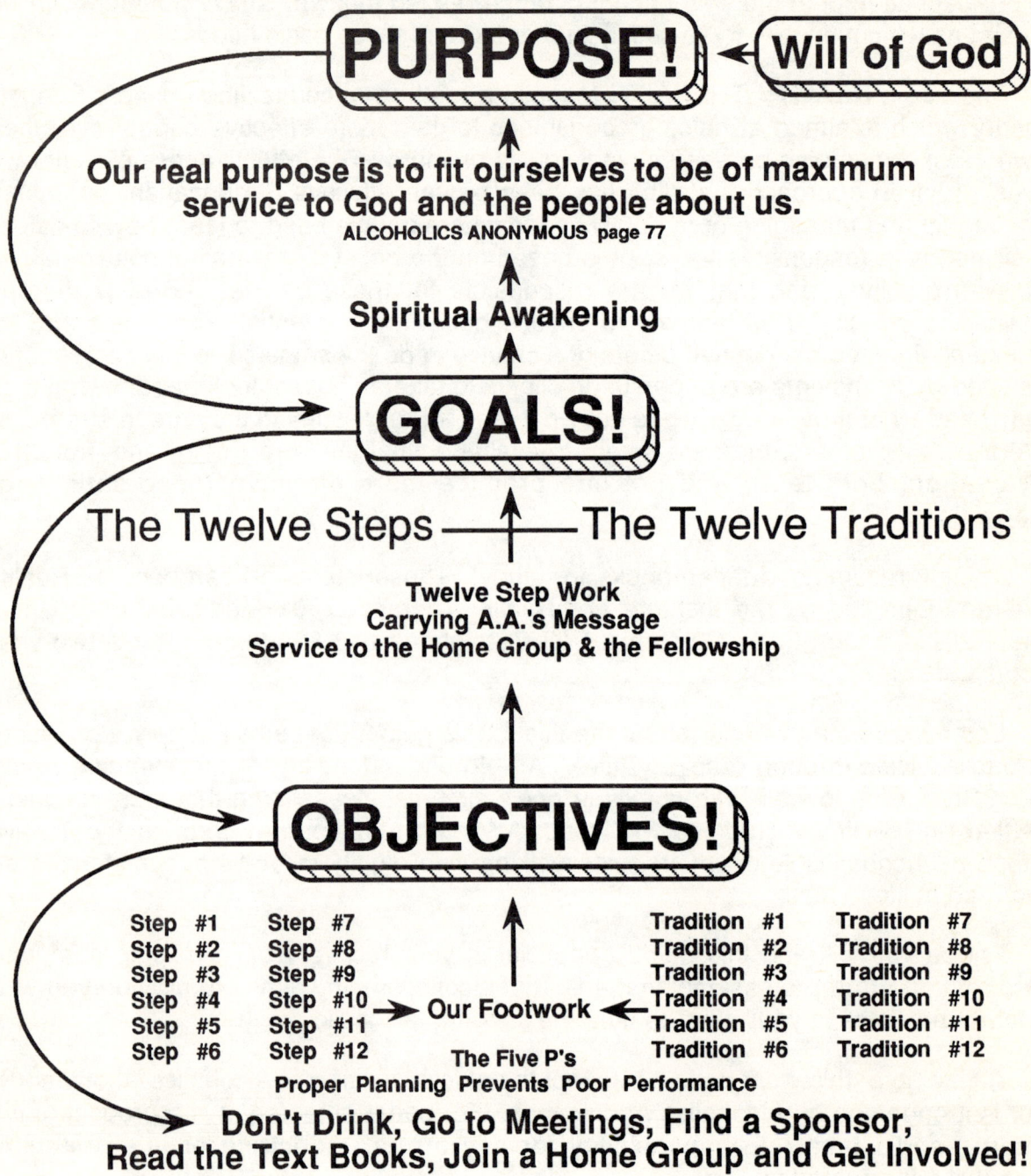

PURPOSE! ← Will of God

Our real purpose is to fit ourselves to be of maximum
service to God and the people about us.
ALCOHOLICS ANONYMOUS page 77

Spiritual Awakening

GOALS!

The Twelve Steps ——— The Twelve Traditions

Twelve Step Work
Carrying A.A.'s Message
Service to the Home Group & the Fellowship

OBJECTIVES!

Step #1	Step #7		Tradition #1	Tradition #7
Step #2	Step #8		Tradition #2	Tradition #8
Step #3	Step #9		Tradition #3	Tradition #9
Step #4	Step #10	→ Our Footwork ←	Tradition #4	Tradition #10
Step #5	Step #11		Tradition #5	Tradition #11
Step #6	Step #12		Tradition #6	Tradition #12

The Five P's
Proper Planning Prevents Poor Performance

**Don't Drink, Go to Meetings, Find a Sponsor,
Read the Text Books, Join a Home Group and Get Involved!**

Organization of the Text of ALCOHOLICS ANONYMOUS

CONTENTS

The Preface and Forewords provide us with basic, but important information. They set the background so we can begin our study of the text.

Our text book is organized in a simple problem–solving fashion. First, we need to know the exact nature of our problem.

Next, we need to know if there is a solution to our problem.

Finally, we need to know how to receive the solution that solves our problem.

The text then has several chapters that show how to handle many life situations. Included are personal stories to help us understand how others solved their problems using the A.A. program.

PREFACE (xi - xii)

1. WHAT IS A TEXT? _____
_____
_____ (xi)

2. A.A. MEETINGS AND THE STORIES IN THE BOOK CAN HELP US SEE
   THREE THINGS. WHAT ARE THEY? A _____
   B _____ C _____ (xii)

FOREWORD TO FIRST EDITION (xiii - xiv)

1. "We, of Alcoholics Anonymous, are more than one hundred men and women
   who have recovered from a seemingly hopeless state of mind and body."
   WHAT IS THIS HOPELESS STATE? _____ (xiii)

2. WHAT IS THE MAIN PURPOSE OF THE BOOK? _____
   _____ (xiii)

FOREWORD TO SECOND EDITION (xv - xxi)

1. WHO HELPED BILL WITH HIS SPIRITUAL EXPERIENCE? _____ (xv, xvi)

2. FROM WHOM DID THE BROKER LEARN THE GRAVE NATURE OF
   ALCOHOLISM ? _____ (xvi)

3. BILL WAS CONVINCED OF THE NEED FOR MORAL INVENTORY,
   CONFESSION OF PERSONALITY DEFECTS, RESTITUTION TO THOSE
   HARMED, HELPFULNESS TO OTHERS, AND THE NECESSITY OF BELIEF
   IN AND DEPENDENCE UPON GOD. WHERE DID THESE TENETS COME
   FROM? _____ (xvi)

4. WHAT IS THE MESSAGE OF A.A.? _____
   _____

   (xvii - xviii - xxi: 58, 79, 60, 58.)

5. PUBLIC ACCEPTANCE OF A.A. GREW BY LEAPS AND BOUNDS FOR TWO
   PRINCIPAL REASONS. WHAT ARE THEY?
   A _____
   B _____ (xx)

FOREWORD TO THIRD EDITION (xxii)

1. THE TWELVE STEPS DO WHAT TO THE PROGRAM? _____
   _____ (xxii)

2. THE TWELVE STEPS TRACE WHAT? _____
   _____
   _____ (xxii)

3. RECOVERY BEGINS WHEN? _____
   _____
   _____ (xxii)

NOTES

THE DOCTOR'S OPINION   Step #1
(xxiii - xxx, 569 - 570)   (12x12, 21 - 24)

1. ON WHAT TWO PLANES DO WE WORK OUT THE SOLUTION?
   A_____ B_____
   EXPLAIN WHAT THIS MEANS: _____
   _____
   _____
   _____
   _____ (xxiv)

2. WHAT NEVER OCCURS IN THE AVERAGE TEMPERATE DRINKER?
   _____ (xxvi)

3. "Men and women drink essentially because they like the effect produced by alcohol." WHAT IS THE EFFECT AND WHY IS THIS IMPORTANT TO KNOW FOR CONTINUED SOBRIETY? A_____
   _____
   B_____
   _____ (xxvi, xxvii)

4. "On the other hand--and strange as this may seem to those who do not understand--once a psychic change has occurred, the very same person who seemed doomed, who had so many problems he despaired of ever solving them, suddenly finds himself easily able to control his desire for alcohol, the only effort necessary being that required to follow a few simple _____." (xxvii)

5. DEFINE PSYCHE: _____ (xxvii)

6. "These men were not drinking to escape; they were drinking to overcome a _____ beyond their mental control."   (xxviii)

7. "All these, and many others, have one symptom in common: they cannot start drinking without developing the _____ _____ _____." (xxviii)

8. DEFINE THE PHENOMENON OF CRAVING: _____
   _____
   _____
   GIVE AN ANALOGY: _____
   EXPLAIN: _____
   _____
   _____
   _____ (xxviii)

9. AFTER WITHDRAWAL FROM ALCOHOL PLUS A DECISION NOT TO START DRINKING AGAIN, WE NO LONGER HAVE A COMPULSION FOR ALCOHOL. TO MAINTAIN OUR ABSTINENCE, WE MUST WORK ON THE OBSESSION OF ALCOHOLISM.   TRUE or FALSE

10. AS WILLIAM JAMES POINTED OUT, THE ONLY DIFFERENCE BETWEEN A SPIRITUAL EXPERIENCE AND A SPIRITUAL AWAKENING IS _____ (569)

11. A SPIRITUAL AWAKENING CHANGES A PERSON IN WHAT THREE AREAS?
    A _____ B _____ C _____ (569)

12. WHAT IS THE ESSENCE OF A SPIRITUAL EXPERIENCE? _____
    _____
    _____
    _____ (569, 570)

13. WHAT WILL KEEP MAN IN EVERLASTING IGNORANCE? _____
    _____
    _____ (570)

14. LITTLE GOOD CAN COME TO AN ALCOHOLIC UNLESS HE FIRST ACCEPTS
    HIS DEVASTATING WEAKNESS AND ALL ITS CONSEQUENCES. EXPLAIN
    WHY: _____
    _____
    _____
    _____
    _____
    _____ (12x12, 21)

15. WHAT IS THE MAIN TAPROOT? _____
    _____ EXPLAIN: _____
    _____
    _____
    _____
    _____ (12x12, 22)

16. ALCOHOL WIELDS A DOUBLE-EDGED SWORD; WHAT ARE THE TWO
    EDGES? EXPLAIN EACH: A _____
    _____
    _____
    B _____
    _____
    _____ (12x12, 22)

17. WHAT SHOULD WE FIRST TELL A PERSON TO WHOM WE SAY THAT THEY
    MAY NOT BE AN ALCOHOLIC, AND PERHAPS THEY SHOULD TRY SOME
    CONTROLLED DRINKING? _____
    _____
    _____
    _____ (12x12, 23)

18. FOR PRACTICAL RESULTS, WHAT DO WE NEED TO PLANT IN THE MIND
    OF AN ALCOHOLIC? WHAT WON'T BE THE SAME AGAIN?
    A _____
    _____
    _____
    B _____
    _____
    _____ (12x12, 23)

NOTES

NOTES

Chapter 1   BILL'S STORY   Step #1
(1 - 16)

1. LOOK FOR THE PROGRESSION OF BILL'S ALCOHOLISM AND GIVE SOME EXAMPLES: _____
   _____
   _____
   _____
   _____ (2-7)

2. "Liquor ceased to be a luxury; it became a necessity."   EXPLAIN THIS IN TERMS OF THE DISEASE CONCEPT OF ALCOHOLISM AND NOTE BILL'S THINKING AFTER THIS: A_____
   _____
   _____
   _____
   B_____
   _____ (5)

3. WHAT WAS BILL'S MOMENT OF CLARITY? WHAT DID HE THEN DO?
   A_____
   B_____ (5)

4. WHAT IS A DEFINITION OF INSANITY? _____
   _____
   _____ (5, 37)

5. DID BILL USE DRUGS? _____ (7)

6. LOCATE IN THE BOOK WHERE BILL WENT INTO THE HOSPITAL FOR THE FIRST TIME? _____
   _____ (7)

7. FIND IN THE BOOK WHERE BILL LEARNED THE NATURE OF ALCOHOLISM. EXPLAIN: _____
   _____
   _____
   WHAT DID HE THEN DO? _____ (7)

8. FIND IN THE BOOK WHERE BILL WENT INTO THE HOSPITAL FOR THE SECOND TIME. NOTICE HIS THINKING. _____
   _____ (7)

9. ON PAGE 8, LOCATE WHERE BILL TOOK STEP ONE. WHAT DID HE DO AFTER STEP ONE? _____ (8)

10. DID FEAR **KEEP** BILL SOBER? _____ (8)

11. BILL'S FRIEND (EBBY) TOLD HIM HOW TWO MEN CARRIED THE MESSAGE TO HIM. THEY TOLD HIM TWO SIMPLE IDEAS, WHAT ARE THEY? A_____
    B_____ (9)

12. WHAT WAS THE POINT BLANK DECLARATION THAT BILL'S FRIEND MADE TO HIM? _____

_____

WHAT FAILED BILL? _____

_____ (11)

13. FIND ON PAGE 12 WHERE BILL TOOK STEP TWO. WHAT DID HE DO AFTER STEP TWO? _____

_____ (12)

14. FIND WHERE BILL WENT INTO THE HOSPITAL FOR THE THIRD TIME.

_____

WHAT DID THEY DO TO HIM THERE? _____

_____ (13)

15. HOW MANY STEPS DID BILL TAKE ON PAGE 13? _____ (13)

16. WHAT ARE THE FOUR ESSENTIAL REQUIREMENTS TO SOBRIETY?
A_____ B_____
C_____ D_____ (13, 14)

17. THESE ESSENTIALS ARE A PROCESS LEADING FROM ADMISSION TO ACCEPTANCE, EXPLAIN. _____

_____

_____

_____

_____

_____

_____

_____ (14)

18. THE FOUR ESSENTIALS PRODUCE TWO PROMISES; WHAT ARE THEY?
A_____
B_____ (14)

19. BILL'S FRIEND EMPHASIZED THE ABSOLUTE NECESSITY OF DEMON-STARTING THESE PRINCIPLES IN ALL HIS AFFAIRS. WHAT ELSE DID HE TELL HIM? _____

_____

_____ (14)

20. BILL SOON FOUND THAT WHEN ALL OTHER MEASURES FAILED, WORK WITH ANOTHER ALCOHOLIC WOULD SAVE THE DAY. IN THE CONTEXT OF BILL'S STORY, WHAT HAD BILL DONE BEFORE THIS TO REALIZE HE NEEDED TO WORK WITH ANOTHER ALCOHOLIC? _____

_____

_____

_____

_____ (15)

21. FAITH HAS TO WORK TWENTY-FOUR HOURS A DAY **IN** AND **THROUGH** US, OR WHAT WILL HAPPEN? _____ _____
EXPLAIN: _____ (16)

NOTES

22

NOTES

1. PAGE 17 USES THE ANALOGY OF THE SHIP TO DEMONSTRATE THE THREE SIDES OF THE A.A. PROGRAM. WHAT ARE THESE THREE COMPONENTS? A_____ B_____ C _____ (17)

2. ON PAGE 18 IS A LIST OF QUALITIES FOR A SPONSOR. HOW MANY ARE THERE? _____ THINK ABOUT EACH.   (18)

3. WHERE IS IT IMPORTANT TO DEMONSTRATE OUR PRINCIPLES? A_____ B_____ C_____ (19)

4.   AS EX-PROBLEM DRINKERS, OUR VERY LIVES DEPEND UPON WHAT? A_____ B_____ (20)

5. WHAT IS ANOTHER PURPOSE OF THE BOOK? _____ _____ (20)

6. THINK ABOUT THE **MODERATE** DRINKER , THE **HARD** DRINKER AND THE **REAL** ALCOHOLIC. EXPLAIN WHY IT IS IMPORTANT TO KNOW THE DIFFERENCE: _____ _____ _____ (20, 21)

7. AT SOME STAGE OF OUR DRINKING WE BEGIN TO LOSE ALL CONTROL OF WHAT? _____ EXPLAIN: _____ _____ (21)

8. AS ALCOHOLISM GROWS WORSE, WHAT MAY COME INTO PLAY? _____ (22)

9. "We are equally positive that once we take alcohol into our system something happens, both in the _____ and _____sense, which makes it virtually impossible to _____." (22, 23)

10. THE MAIN PROBLEM OF THE ALCOHOLIC CENTERS IN THE _____ RATHER THAN IN THE_____ (23)

11. "There is the obsession that somehow, someday, they will beat the game." EXPLAIN: _____ _____ _____ _____ (23)

12. "IF YOU DON'T REMEMBER YOUR LAST DRUNK, YOU HAVEN'T HAD IT." THIS STATEMENT IS COMMONLY HEARD IN A.A. MEETINGS. IS THIS A TRUE STATEMENT? _____ EXPLAIN: _____ _____ _____ _____ (24)

13. THERE ARE THREE COMPONENTS IN THE SOLUTION FOR ALCOHOLISM, WHAT ARE THEY?   A _____

    B _____

    C _____ (25)

14. WHAT ARE OUR TWO CHOICES IF WE ARE ALCOHOLIC?   A _____

    _____

    _____

    _____

    B _____

    _____ (25)

15. A NOTED PSYCHIATRIST PROVIDED THE SOLUTION TO ALCOHOLISM. WHO WAS HE AND WHAT WAS HIS SOLUTION?   A _____

    B _____ (26, 27)

16. "Here and there, once in a while, alcoholics have had what are called vital spiritual experiences."   THEY CHANGE A PERSON IN THREE AREAS. WHAT ARE THESE AREAS?   A _____

    B _____   C _____ (27)

17. IF WE WANT TO FORM A RELATIONSHIP WITH OUR CREATOR UPON SIMPLE AND UNDERSTANDABLE TERMS WE HAVE TO BE _____ AND _____ ENOUGH TO _____ (28)

18. "Not all of us join _____ _____ , but most of us favor such membership."   (28)

19. "Further on, _____ - _____ _____ are given showing how we recovered."   (29)

25

NOTES

NOTES

1. EXPLAIN THE STATEMENT,   "someday he will control and enjoy his drinking":
    _____
    _____
    _____
    _____ (30)

2. DEFINE COMPULSION: _____
    _____

    OBSESSION: _____
    _____

    ILLUSION: _____
    _____

    DELUSION: _____
    _____ (30)

3. WHAT IS A BETTER SUMMARY OF STEP ONE? _____
    _____
    _____
    _____ (30)

4. MANY ALCOHOLICS WILL TRY TO PROVE THEMSELVES EXCEPTIONS TO
    THE RULE. WHAT DO THEY USE FOR THIS AND WHAT IS ANOTHER
    WORD FOR IT? A _____ B _____ (31)

5. HOW MAY YOU DIAGNOSE YOURSELF AN ALCOHOLIC? _____
    _____ (31, 32)

6.   WHY CAN'T AN ALCOHOLIC DO THE ABOVE? _____
    _____ (31)

7. EARLIER IN THEIR DRINKING CAREERS, COULD MOST ALCOHOLICS
    HAVE STOPPED THEIR DRINKING? _____ (32)

8. TO WHAT BELIEF DO MOST ALCOHOLICS FALL VICTIM? _____
    _____
    _____ (32)

9. WHAT IS ANOTHER NAME FOR THE OBSESSION OF ALCOHOLISM?
    _____ (33)

10. DOES ALCOHOL SEEM TO AFFECT WOMEN SOMEWHAT DIFFERENTLY
    THAN MEN? _____ (33)

11. IF YOU'VE ENTERED THE DANGEROUS AREA OF ALCOHOLISM, YOU
    WON'T BE ABLE TO LEAVE LIQUOR ALONE FOR ONE YEAR.
                                     TRUE or FALSE   (34)

12. WHAT IS THE BAFFLING FEATURE OF ALCOHOLISM? _____
    _____
    _____
    _____ (34)

13. WHAT IS THE CRUX OF THE PROBLEM? _____
_____
_____ (35)

14. DESCRIBE HOW JIM FELT BEFORE HE DRANK? _____
_____
_____
_____ (36)

15. WHAT WAS JIM'S OBSESSION? _____
_____
_____
_____ (36)

16. FIND WHERE JIM'S CRAVING TAKES OVER? _____
_____
_____
_____ (36, 37)

17. GIVE A DEFINITION OF INSANITY. _____
_____
_____
_____

EXPLAIN: _____
_____
_____
_____

WHAT ONE WORD DO WE CALL THIS? _____ (37)

18. "There inevitably ran some _____ _____
_____ for taking the first drink."   (37)

19. WHAT DOES THE JAY-WALKER REPRESENT? _____
EXPLAIN: _____
_____
_____
_____
_____ (37, 38)

20. INTELLECT AND SELF-KNOWLEDGE ARE IMPORTANT, BUT CAN AN
ALCOHOLIC STOP DRINKING ON THAT BASIS ALONE? _____ (38, 39)

21. DESCRIBE HOW FRED FELT BEFORE HE DRANK? _____
_____
_____
_____
_____ (39, 40)

22. WHAT WAS FRED'S OBSESSION? _____
_____
_____
_____
_____ (41)

29

23. FIND WHERE FRED'S CRAVING TOOK OVER? _____
_____
_____
_____ (41)

24. JIM FELT BAD IN SOBRIETY AND FRED FELT GOOD IN SOBRIETY. WHAT
HAPPENED TO BOTH? _____
EXPLAIN WHAT THIS MEANS: _____
_____
_____
_____
_____ (36, 41)

25. WHAT TWO QUESTIONS MUST AN ALCOHOLIC CONCEDE?
A _____
B _____
EXPLAIN: _____
_____
_____
_____
_____ (42)

26. WHAT WILL SOLVE ALL OUR PROBLEMS? _____
_____ (42)

27. WHO WILL PROVIDE OUR DEFENSE AGAINST THE FIRST DRINK?
_____
_____
_____ (43)

NOTES

Chapter 4   WE AGNOSTIC   Step #2
(44 - 57)   (12x12, 25 - 33)

1. FIND ANOTHER TEST TO SEE IF YOU'RE AN ALCOHOLIC.

   _____
   _____
   _____

   EXPLAIN: _____
   _____
   _____
   _____
   _____ (44)

2. "Lack of power, that was our dilemma."   EXPLAIN WHAT THIS MEANS?

   _____
   _____
   _____
   _____
   _____ (45)

3. WHAT IS THE OBJECT OF THE BOOK?_____
   _____ (45)

4. WILL THE OBJECT OF THE BOOK SOLVE OUR PROBLEM? _____ (45)

5. FIND TWO PROMISES ON PAGE 46. A _____
   _____
   _____
   _____
   B _____
   _____
   _____
   _____ (46)

6. TO SET OUR CORNERSTONE IN PLACE, WHAT DO WE NEED TO ASK
   OURSELVES? _____
   _____
   _____ (47)

7. WHAT IS THE GREAT PERSUADER? _____ (48)

8. SHOULD WE LAY ASIDE PREJUDICE, EVEN AGAINST ORGANIZED
   RELIGION? _____ (49)

9. PEOPLE OF FAITH POSSESS THREE THINGS. WHAT ARE THEY?
   A _____
   _____
   B _____
   _____
   C _____
   _____ (49)

10. FIND A PROMISE ON PAGE 50. _____
_____
_____ (50)

11. EXPLAIN HOW COLUMBUS REPRESENTS AN APPLICATION OF THE FOUR
ESSENTIALS FOR ACCEPTANCE. _____
_____
_____
_____
_____
_____
_____
_____ (13, 14, 51, 52)

12. IF WE ARE TO SOLVE OUR PROBLEMS, WHAT MUST WE DO? _____
_____ (52)

13. WE WERE GIVEN THE POWER TO REASON. WHAT ARE WE TO EXAMINE
WITH IT? _____
_____ (53)

14. "When we became alcoholics, crushed by a _____ – _____ crisis we
could not postpone or evade, we had to fearlessly _____ the proposition
that either _____ is everything or else He is nothing. _____ either is,
or He isn't. What was our choice to be?"   (53)

15. WHAT IS THE DESIRED SHORE AND WHAT WILL TAKE US PART OF THE
WAY? A_____ B_____ (53)

16. "But where and how were we to find this power?" (45) WHERE? _____
_____
HOW? _____
_____ (55)

17. WHAT IS THE GREAT REALITY? _____ (55)

18. ON PAGE 55 IS THIS PROMISE: "With this attitude you cannot fail." WHAT
ARE THE REQUIREMENTS (CONDITIONS) TO RECEIVING THIS PROMISE?
A_____
B_____
C_____ (55)

19. GIVE A DEFINITION OF SANITY. _____
_____
_____
EXPLAIN: _____
_____
_____
_____
_____ (57)

20. WHAT ARE THE THREE ELEMENTS OF HEALING?

A _____

_____

B _____

_____

C _____

_____ (57)

21. HAS GOD RESTORED US TO OUR RIGHT MINDS? _____ (57)

22. WHAT IS THE PROMISE ON PAGE 57 AND HOW DO WE RECEIVE IT?

A _____

_____

B _____

_____ (57)

23. YOUR HIGHER POWER WILL REMOVE THE OBSESSION OF ALCOHOLISM, BUT WHAT STATE MUST YOU BE IN? _____ (12x12, 25)

24. TO ACQUIRE IT (belief in a Higher Power), "...I had only to stop _____ and _____ the rest of A.A.'s program as _____ as I could." (12x12, 27)

25. HUMILITY AND INTELLECT CAN BE COMPATIBLE, PROVIDED WE PLACE HUMILITY _____ (12x12, 30)

26. WHAT IS THE OUTSTANDING CHARACTERISTIC OF MANY ALCOHOLICS?

_____ (12x12, 31)

27. "Belief meant _____ not _____." (12x12, 31)

28. HUMILITY IS: "To those who have made progress in A.A., it amounts to a clear recognition of what and who we really are, followed by a sincere attempt to become what we could be." (12x12, 58) "True _____ and an open _____ can lead us to faith, and every A.A. meeting is an assurance that God will restore us to sanity if we rightly relate ourselves to Him." (12x12, 33)

29. "Religion says the existence of God can be proved; the agnostic says it *can't* be proved; and the atheist claims, proof of the nonexistence of God." (12x12, 28)

IN A.A. WE LEARN TO BRING OUR INTENTIONS AND OUR ACTIONS INTO ALIGNMENT, AND THEN THE FEELINGS FOLLOW.

A **TRUE BELIEVER** RELIES ON GOD AND HIS ACTIONS SHOW IT.

AN **ATHEIST** DOESN'T BELIEVE IN GOD AND HIS ACTIONS SHOW IT.

AN **AGNOSTIC** PROFESSES DISBLIEF IN GOD BUT HIS ACTIONS SHOW HE RELIES ON HIM. OR AN **AGNOSTIC** PROFESSES BELIEF IN GOD BUT HIS ACTIONS SHOW HE DOESN'T RELY ON HIM.

AGREE or DISAGREE

NOTES

1. WHAT IS THE PROMISE ON PAGE 58? _____
   _____
   _____ (58)

2. WHEN USED AS AN ADJECTIVE, "RIGOROUS" MEANS "CONFORMING TO
   OR AGREEING WITH FACT." EXPLAIN WHAT RIGOROUS HONESTY
   MEANS? _____
   _____
   _____
   _____ (58)

3. DEFINE HONESTY: _____ (58)

4. IF YOU HAVE DECIDED YOU WANT A _____ AND
   ARE WILLING TO WORK THE _____ TO RECEIVE THAT _____
   THEN YOU ARE READY FOR STEP _____ .   (58, 79, 60, 58)

5. WHAT IS THE TURNING POINT? _____ (59)

6. "Here are the steps we took, which are suggested as a program of recovery."
   THIS SEEMS TO SAY THE ENTIRE PROGRAM IS SUGGESTED, NOT THE
   STEPS. IF YOU WANT A.A.'s PROGRAM OF RECOVERY, THEN THE STEPS
   ARE A MUST.   TRUE or FALSE   (59)

7. ON PAGE 60 PARTS (a), (b) AND (c) REPRESENT WHAT TWO THINGS?
   A _____ B _____ (60)

8. THERE ARE EIGHT **GENERAL** REQUIREMENTS FOR STEP THREE.
   NUMBERS ONE AND TWO ARE ON PAGE 60, NUMBERS TWO (#2 is
   restated in a different form) AND THREE ARE ON PAGE 62, AND
   NUMBERS FOUR THROUGH EIGHT ARE ON PAGE 63. LIST ALL EIGHT.
   A _____
   _____
   B _____
   _____
   C _____
   _____
   D _____
   _____
   E _____
   _____
   F _____
   _____
   G _____
   _____
   H _____
   _____ (60, 62, 63)

9. "Is he not a victim of the _____ that he can wrest satisfaction
   and happiness out of this world if he only _____ well?"   (61)

10. WHAT IS THE ROOT OF OUR TROUBLES? _____ (62)

11. THE ROOTS OF SELF MUST RESIDE IN SOME SUBSTANCE. WHAT IS THE SUBSTANCE OF SELF THAT CAUSES SELF-CENTEREDNESS?

   _____

   _____

   _____ (12x12, 35, 36) (62, 64, 65)

12. "The keystone of the new and triumphant arch through which we passed to freedom." THIS IS A SIMPLE IDEA, BASED ON THE NATURE OF ALCOHOLISM, THE SOLUTION, AND HOW TO RECEIVE THE SOLUTION. STEP THREE IS A DECISION TO _____ _____ _____ (62, 64)

13. LIST THE NINE PROMISES ON PAGE 63?

   A _____

   _____

   B _____

   _____

   C _____

   _____

   D _____

   _____

   E _____

   _____

   F _____

   _____

   G _____

   _____

   H _____

   _____

   I _____

   _____ (63)

14. WHAT IS THE THIRD STEP PRAYER? _____

   _____

   _____

   _____

   _____

   _____

   _____ (63)

15. "All we need is a key, and the _____ to swing the door open. There is only one key, and it is called _____." (12x12, 34)

16. "In the first two Steps we were engaged in _____." (12x12, 34)

17. "Isn't it true that in all matters touching upon alcohol, each of them has decided to turn his or her life over to the _____ , protection, and guidance of Alcoholics Anonymous?" (12x12, 35)

   IF WE GO UNDER THE **CARE** OF GOD, IN TIME IT WILL PRODUCE GOD'S **WILL** FOR US. "Our real purpose is to fit ourselves to be of maximum service to _____ and the _____ about us." (77)

18. "But suppose that _____ still cries out, as it certainly will, 'yes, respecting alcohol, I guess I have to be dependent upon A.A., but in all other matters I must still maintain my independence....' " (12x12, 35, 36)
WE BEGIN TO SEE THAT SELF-CENTEREDNESS (root) COMES FROM THE INSTINCTS (cause) WHICH MAKE UP SELF OR THE PERSON.

19. "How persistently we claim the right to decide all by ourselves just what we shall _____ and just how we shall _____." (12x12, 37)

PAGES 85, 86, 87 IN THE BIG BOOK, ALCOHOLICS ANONYMOUS, ADVISES US TO ASK GOD TO DIRECT OUR THINKING AND OUR ACTIONS. FROM WHAT WE ARE LEARNING, IT SEEMS THAT OUR **WILL** IS OUR **THINKING,** AND OUR **LIVES** ARE OUR **INSTINCTS** (causes) THAT WE TAKE ACTION ON (conditions). (85, 86, 87)

20. "So it is by circumstance rather than by any _____ that we have been driven to A.A., have _____ _____ , have acquired the rudiments of faith, and now want to make a _____ to turn our will and our lives over to a Higher Power." (12x12, 38)

21. WHAT IS THE CHIEF SOURCE OF OUR STRENGTH? _____
_____
_____ (12x12, 38, 39)

22. "All of the Twelve Steps _____ sustained and personal exertion to conform to their principles and so, we trust, to God's will." (12x12, 40)

23. WHAT IS OUR WHOLE TROUBLE? WHAT ARE WE TO DO WITH IT?
A._____
B._____ (12x12, 40)

24. WHAT ARE WE TO DO IN ALL TIMES OF EMOTIONAL DISTURBANCE OR INDECISION? _____
_____
_____
_____
_____
_____
_____
_____ (12x12, 41)

NOTES

1. "Our _____ was but a symptom. So we had to get down to _____ and _____." (64)

2. "One object is to _____ damaged or _____ goods, to get rid of them _____ and without _____." (64)

3. "Creation gave us _____ for a purpose." (12x12, 42)

4. "Yet these _____ , so necessary for our existence, often far exceed their proper functions. Powerfully, blindly, many times subtly, they drive us, dominate us, and insist upon ruling our lives." (12x12, 42)

    "Nearly every serious emotional problem can be seen as a case of misdirected _____. When that happens, our great natural assets, the _____ , have turned into physical and mental liabilities." (12x12, 42)

    "Alcoholics especially should be able to see that _____ run wild in themselves is the underlying cause of their destructive drinking." (12x12, 44)

    "Using his best judgment of what has been right and what has been wrong, he might make a rough survey of his conduct with respect to his primary _____ for **sex**, **security**, and **society**." (Emphasis added) (12x12, 50)

    "Since most of us are born with an abundance of _____ _____ , it isn't strange that we often let these far exceed their intended purpose. When they **drive us blindly**, or we **willfully demand** that they supply us with more **satisfactions or pleasures** than are possible or due us, that is the point at which we depart from the degree of perfection that God wishes for us here on earth. That is the measure of our _____ _____ , or, if you wish, of our sins." (Emphasis added) (12x12, 65)

5. "At this stage of the inventory proceedings, our **sponsors** come to the rescue. They can do this, for they are the carriers of A.A.'s tested experience with Step Four. They comfort the melancholy one by first showing him that his case is not strange or different, that his character defects are probably not more numerous or worse than those of anyone else in A.A. This the sponsor promptly proves by talking freely and easily, and without exhibitionism, about his own defects, past and present. This calm, yet realistic, stocktaking is immensely reassuring. The _____ probably points out that the newcomer has some assets which can be noted along with his liabilities. This tends to clear away morbidity and encourage balance. As soon as he begins to be more **objective**, the newcomer can fearlessly, rather than fearfully, look at his own_____." (Emphasis added) (12x12, 46)

RESENTMENTS   FEAR   SEX/HARMS

CONDITIONS OR BEHAVIOR

"Our liquor was but a symptom. So we had to get down to causes and conditions."
ALCOHOLICS ANONYMOUS, page 64

CONDITIONS OR BEHAVIOR

USEFULNESS: FEELING GOOD AND THE BEHAVIOR ISN'T HARMFUL TO SELF OR OTHERS

WE PAUSE WHEN AGITATED OR DOUBTFUL

THINKING OR THE COGNITIVE PROCESSING OF THE BODY'S SENSES

CHARACTER DEFECTS: MAY FEEL BAD AND THE BEHAVIOR CAN BE HARMFUL TO SELF AND OTHERS

SEVEN DEADLY SINS
Pride, Greed, Lust, Anger, Gluttony, Envy, Sloth

ACTING DIRECTLY ON THE FEAR OR FEELINGS COMING FROM THE INSTINCTS

SELFISHNESS SELF-CENTERED, THE ROOT OF OUR TROUBLES

F E A R
OR THE FEELING OF FEAR

SOCIAL
COMPANIONSHIP, PRESTIGE, SELF-ESTEEM, PERSONAL RELATIONSHIPS AMBITIONS

— SELF —

SECURITY
MATERIAL, EMOTIONAL, AMBITIONS

— SELF —

SEX
ACCEPTABLE, HIDDEN, BEING OPEN, INTIMATE, AMBITIONS

— SELF —

SURVIVAL
PHYSICAL SURVIVAL OF THE BODY

CAUSES   **CAUSES**   **CAUSES**

SOCIAL INSTINCT	SECURITY INSTINCT	SEX INSTINCT	SURVIVAL INSTINCT
COMPANIONSHIP: Wanting to belong or to be accepted. PRESTIGE: Wanting to be recognized, or to be accepted as a leader. SELF-ESTEEM: What we think of ourselves. PRIDE: An excessive and unjustified opinion of oneself, either positive(self-love) or negative (self-hate). PERSONAL RELATIONSHIPS: Our relations with other human beings and the world around us. AMBITIONS: Our plans to gain acceptance, power, recognition. POWER: Learning, money. BELONGING: Love, friends. FREEDOM: Choices. FUN: Sports, hobbies.	MATERIAL: Wanting money, building, property, clothing, etc. in order to be secure in the future. EMOTIONAL: Based upon our needs for another person or persons. Some tend to dominate, some are overly dependent on others. AMBITION: Our plans to gain material wealth, or to dominate, or to depend upon others. POWER: Learning, money. BELONGING: Love, friends. FREEDOM: Choices. FUN: Sports, hobbies.	PHYSICAL and PSYCHOLOGICAL ACCEPTABLE: Our sex lives as accepted by Society, God's principles or Our own principles. HIDDEN: Our sex lives that are contrary to either Society, God's principles or Our own principles. AMBITIONS: Our plans regarding our sex lives, either acceptable or hidden. POWER: Learning, money. BELONGING: Love, friends. FREEDOM: Choices. FUN: Sports, hobbies.	PHYSICAL: The body's need for nourishment, exercise and rest. PSYCHOLOGY: The mind's need for mental nourishment, exercise and rest.

6. "By now the newcomer has probably arrived at the following conclusions: that his character defects, representing _____ gone astray, have been the primary cause of his drinking and his failure at life; that unless he is now willing to work hard at the elimination of the worst of these defects, both **sobriety** and **peace of mind** will still elude him; that all the faulty foundation of his life will have to be torn out and built anew on bedrock. Now willing to commence the search for his own **defects**, he will ask, 'Just how do I go about this? *How* do I take inventory of myself?' " (Emphasis added)

(12x12, 50)

WE LOOK AT - RESENTMENTS - FEARS - SEX   (64, 67, 68)

7. "First, we searched out the flaws in our make-up which _____ our failure."

(64)

8. "**Resentment is the 'number one' offender**. It destroys more alcoholics than anything else. From it stem all forms of _____ disease, for we have been not only mentally and physically ill, we have been spiritually sick. When the spiritual malady is overcome, we straighten out _____ and _____." (Emphasis added)

(64)

9. "In dealing with resentments, we set them on _____." (64)

10. "We listed **people**, **institutions** or **principles** with whom we were _____." START WITH TODAY'S MEMORIES AND WORK BACKWARD FROM THERE. (COLUMN #1 - I'm Resentful At:) (Emphasis added)

(64)

11. "We asked ourselves why we were _____." (COLUMN #2 - The Cause:)

(64)

12. "In most cases it was found that our self-esteem (social), our pocketbooks (security), our ambitions (in all three instincts), our personal relationships (including sex) were _____ or _____." (COLUMN #3 - Which Part of Self is Affected?)

(64, 65)

13. "We went back through our lives. Nothing counted but thoroughness and honesty. When we were finished we _____ it carefully." (Review List: the start of Column #4)

(65)

14. "We turned back to the list, for it held the key to the future. We were prepared to look at it from an entirely different angle. We began to see that the world and its people really _____ us. In that state, the wrong-doing of others, fancied or real, had power to actually kill. How could we escape? We saw that these resentments must be mastered, but how? We could not wish them away any more than alcohol."

(66)

15. "This was our course: We realized that the people who wronged us were perhaps _____ sick. Though we did not like their symptoms and the way these disturbed us, they, like ourselves, were sick too." **We asked God to help us show them the same tolerance, pity, and patience that we would cheerfully grant a sick friend. When a person offended we said to ourselves, 'This is a sick man. How can I be helpful to him? God save me from being angry. Thy will be done.' " (Prayer)** (Emphasis added) (66, 67)

16. "Referring to our _____ again. Putting out of our minds the wrongs others had done, we resolutely looked for our own mistakes. Where had we been selfish, dishonest, self-seeking and frightened? Though a situation had not been entirely our fault, we tried to **disregard** the other person involved entirely. Where were we to blame?" (Emphasis added)
(Column 4 - Symptom of the Nature:) (67)

17. "The inventory was ours, not the other man's. When we saw our **faults** we _____ them." (Emphasis added)
(Column #5 - Refer To List, Look For Nature, Wrong or Instincts:) (67)
NATURE: "an inner force or the sum of such forces in an individual."
WRONG: "not according to the moral standard or not in accordance with one's needs , intent, or expectations." (Webster's New Collegiate Dictionary)

18. "We placed them before us in black and white. We admitted our _____ honestly and were willing to set these matters straight."
(# 6 on Inventory Guide) (67)

19. "Our egomania digs _____ disastrous pitfalls. Either we insist upon _____ the people we know, or we _____ upon them far too much." (12x12, 53)

20. "Therefore, no peace was to be had unless we could find a means of _____ these demands. The difference between a demand and a simple request is plain to anyone." (12x12, 76)

REVIEW THESE QUESTIONS FOR RESENTMENTS, BEFORE YOU START.
1. Do I insist upon dominating the people I know?
2. Do I depend upon them far too much? If we lean too heavily on people, they will sooner or later fail us, for they are human, too, and cannot possibly meet our incessant demands. In this way our insecurity grows and festers.
3. Do I habitually try to manipulate others to have my own willful desires? They revolt and resist us heavily. Then we develop hurt feelings, a sense of persecution, and a desire to retaliate.
4. Do I redouble my efforts at control, and continue to fail, then my suffering becomes acute and constant?
5. Do I seek to be one in a family, to be a friend among friends, to be a worker among workers, to be a useful member of society?
6. Do I to struggle to the top of the heap, or to hide underneath it? (12x12, 53)

INVENTORY FOR RESENTMENTS

1. In dealing with resentments we set them on paper. We listed People, Institutions, or Principles with whom we were angry. (Start with today's memories and work backward from there. Complete Column 1 from top to bottom. Do nothing on Columns 2, 3, 4, or 5 and instruction # 6 until Column 1 is complete.)

2. We asked ourselves why we were angry? (Complete Column 2 from top to bottom. Do nothing on Columns 3, 4, or 5 and instruction # 6 until Column 2 is complete.)

3. On our grudge list we set opposite each name our injuries. Was it our self-esteem, our security, our ambitions, our personal or sex relations which had been interfered with? (Complete each column within Column 3 going from top to bottom. Starting with the Self-Esteem and finishing with the Sexual Ambitions Column. Do nothing on Columns 4, or 5 and instruction # 6 until Column 3 is complete.)

4. Referring to our list again. Putting out of our minds the wrongs others had done, we resolutely looked for our own mistakes. Where had we been selfish, dishonest, self-seeking and frightened and inconsiderate? (Asking ourselves the above questions we complete each column within Column 4. Do nothing on Column 5 or instruction # 6 until Column 4 is complete.)

5. The Inventory was ours, not the others man's. When we saw our faults we listed them. By now we have probably arrived at the following conclusion: that our Character Defects represent Instincts gone astray. Look for the Nature or the Cause, which is one or more of the Instincts causing the condition. (Looking for the affected Instincts, we complete each column within Column 5. Do nothing about instruction # 6 until Column 5 is complete.)

6. Reading from left to right we now see the resentment (Column 1), the cause (Column 2), the part of self that had been affected (Column 3), the symptom of the Nature (Column 4), and the Exact Nature or Cause of Behavior; which are the INSTINCTS (Column 5).

	COLUMN 1 I'm Resentful At:	COLUMN 2 The Cause:	COLUMN 3 WHICH PART OF SELF IS AFFECTED? Social Instinct — Self-Esteem	Personal Relationships	Ambitions	Security Instinct — Material	Emotional	Ambitions	Sex Instinct — Hidden Sex Relations	Acceptable Sex Relations	Ambitions / Prayer	COLUMN 4 What is the Symptom of the Nature of our wrongs, faults, mistakes, defect, shortcomings. — Selfish	Dishonest	Self-Seeking Frightened	Inconsiderate	COLUMN 5 What is the exact NATURE (Instincts) of our defects, or the CAUSE of behavior — Social	Security	Sexual
1																		
2																		
3																		
4																		
5																		
6																		
7																		
8																		
9																		
10																		
11																		
12																		

21. NOTICE THAT WORD **FEAR**, THIS SHORT WORD SOMEHOW TOUCHES
ABOUT _____ _____ OF OUR LIVES.   (67)

22. "We reviewed our fears thoroughly. We put them on _____ , even
though we had no resentment in connection with them."   (68)
START WITH TODAY'S MEMORIES AND WORK BACKWARD FROM THERE.
(Column #1 - I'm Fearful Of:)   (68)

23. "We asked ourselves _____ we had them."
(Column #2 - Why Do I Have The Fear?)   (68)

24. "Wasn't it because _____ failed us? Self-reliance was
good as far as it went, but it didn't go far enough. Some of us once had great
self-confidence, but it didn't fully solve the fear problem, or any other. When it
made us cocky, it was worse."
(Column #3 - Which Part of Self is Affected?)   (68)

25. "Just to the extent that we do as we think He would have us, and humbly
_____ on Him, does He enable us to match calamity with serenity."
(Column #4 - Symptom of the Nature:)   (68)

26. "The verdict of the ages is that faith means _____. All
men of faith have courage. They trust their God. We never apologize for God.
Instead we let Him demonstrate, through us, what He can do."
(Column #5 - Look For Nature, Wrong or Instincts:)   (68)

27. "We ask Him to remove our fear and direct our _____
to what He would have us be."
(Prayer)   (68)

28. "At once, we commence to _____ fear."
(# 6 on Inventory Guide)   (68)

29. "We are in the world to play the role He assigns." WHAT IS THAT ROLE?

    _____
    _____
    _____
    _____
    _____
    _____ (68, 77)

30. LIST THE SEVEN DEADLY SINS (DEFECTS)? A_____
    B_____ C_____ D_____
    E_____ F_____ G_____ (12x12, 48)

31. WHAT IS THE BASIC BREEDER OF MOST HUMAN DIFFICULTIES AND THE
CHIEF BLOCK TO TRUE PROGRESS? _____ (12x12, 48, 49)

32. THE _____ _____ _____ ARE THE
TERMITES THAT CEASELESSLY DEVOUR THE FOUNDATIONS OF
WHATEVER SORT OF LIFE WE TRY TO BUILD.   (12x12, 48, 49)

33. "The verdict of the ages is that faith means courage. All men of faith have courage." THIS INVOLVES FOUR IDEAS. WHAT ARE THEY?

A _____

B _____

C _____
_____

D _____
_____ (68)

34. WHAT ARE THE FIRST FRUITS OF STEP FOUR? A _____
_____

B _____
_____

TO RECEIVE THIS, WE MUST: _____
_____. (12x12, 50)

REVIEW THESE QUESTIONS FOR FEARS, BEFORE YOU START.
1. In addition to my drinking problem, what character defects contributed to my financial instability?
2. Did fear and inferiority about my fitness for my job destroy my confidence and fill me with conflict?
3. Did I try to cover up those feelings of inadequacy by bluffing, cheating, lying, or evading responsibility?
4. Did I gripe that others failed to recognize my truly exceptional abilities?
5. Did I overvalue myself and play the big shot?
6. Did I have such unprincipled ambition that I double-crossed and undercut my associates?
7. Was I extravagant?
8. Did I recklessly borrow money, caring little whether it was repaid or not?
9. Was I a pinchpenny, refusing to support my family properly?
10. Did I cut corners financially?
11. What about the "quick money" deals, the stock market, and the races?
12. Looking at both past and present, what sex situations have caused me anxiety, bitterness, frustration, or depression?
13. Appraising each situation fairly, can I see where I have been at fault?
14. Did these perplexities beset me because of selfishness or unreasonable demands?
15. If my disturbance was seemingly caused by the behavior of others, why do I lack the ability to accept conditions I cannot change? These are the sort of fundamental inquiries that can disclose the source of my discomfort and indicate whether I may be able to **alter my own conduct** and so **adjust myself serenely to self-discipline**.
16. I can ask myself to what extent have my own mistakes fed my gnawing anxieties.
17. And if the actions of others are part of the cause, what can I do about that?
18. If I am unable to change the present state of affairs, am I willing to take the measures necessary to shape my life to conditions as they are? Questions like these, more of which will come to mind easily in each individual case, will help turn up the root causes. (12x12, 51, 52, 53)

INVENTORY FOR FEARS

1. In dealing with fears we set them on paper. We listed People, Institutions, or Principles with whom we were fearful. (Start with today's memories and work backward from there. Complete Column 1 from top to bottom. Do nothing on Columns 2, 3, 4, or 5 and instruction # 6 until Column 1 is complete.)

2. We asked ourselves why do we have the fear? (Complete Column 2 from top to bottom. Do nothing on Columns 3, 4, or 5 and instruction # 6 until Column 2 is complete.)

3. Which part of self caused the fear. Was it our self-esteem, our security, our ambitions, our personal or sex relations which had been interfered with? (Complete each column within Column 3 going from top to bottom. Starting with the Self-Esteem and finishing with the Sexual Ambitions Column. Do nothing on Columns 4, or 5 and instruction # 6 until Column 3 is complete.)

4. Referring to our list again. Putting out of our minds the wrongs others had done, we resolutely looked for our own mistakes. Where had we been selfish, dishonest, self-seeking and frightened and inconsiderate? (Asking ourselves the above questions we complete each column within Column 4. Do nothing on Column 5 or instruction # 6 until Column 4 is complete.)

5. The Inventory was ours, not the others man's. When we saw our faults we listed them. By now we have probably arrived at the following conclusion: that our Character Defects represent Instincts gone astray. Look for the Nature or the Cause, which is one or more of the Instincts causing the condition. (Looking for the affected Instincts, we complete each column within Column 5. Do nothing about instruction # 6 until Column 5 is complete.)

6. Reading from left to right we now see the fear (Column 1), why we have the fear (Column 2), the part of self that caused the fear (Column 3), the symptom of the Nature (Column 4), and the Exact Nature or Cause of the Fear and Behavior; which are the INSTINCTS (Column 5).

| | COLUMN 1 | COLUMN 2 | COLUMN 3 — WHICH PART OF SELF IS AFFECTED? | | | | | | | | | COLUMN 4 — What is the Symptom of the Nature of our wrongs, faults, mistakes, defect, shortcomings. | | | | COLUMN 5 — What is the exact NATURE (Instincts) of our defects, or the CAUSE of behavior | | |
| | | | Social Instinct | | | Security Instinct | | | Sex Instinct | | | | | | | | | |
	I'm Fearful Of:	Why Do I Have The Fear?	Self-Esteem	Personal Relationships	Ambitions	Material	Emotional	Ambitions	Hidden Sex Relations	Acceptable Sex Relations	Ambitions	Selfish	Dishonest	Self-Seeking Frightened	Inconsiderate	Social	Security	Sexual
1																		P
2																		r a y e r
3																		
4																		
5																		
6																		
7																		
8																		
9																		
10																		
11																		
12																		

35. Now about **SEX**. "Many of us needed an overhauling there. But above all, we tried to be _____ on this question." (68)

36. "We reviewed our own _____ over the years past..... Whom had we hurt?" (69)
START WITH TODAY'S MEMORIES AND WORK BACKWARD FROM THERE.
(Column #1 - Whom Did I Hurt?) (69)

37. "Did we unjustifiably arouse jealousy, suspicion or bitterness? Where were we at _____. What should we have done instead? We got this all down on paper and looked at it."
(Column #2 - What Did I Do?) (69)

38. "We all have sex problems." "In this way we tried to shape a _____ and sound ideal for our future sex life."
(Column #3 - Which Part of Self is Affected?) (69)

39. "Where had we been selfish, dishonest, or inconsiderate?" "We subjected each relation to the test--was it _____ or_____?"
(Column #4 - Symptom of the Nature:) (69)

40. "We asked God to mold our _____ and help us to live up to them."
(Prayer) (69)

41. "We remembered always that our sex powers were _____-given and therefore good, neither to be used lightly or selfishly nor to be despised and loathed. Whatever our ideal turns out to be, we must be willing to grow toward it."
(Column #5 - Look For Nature, Wrong or Instincts:) (69)

42. "We must be willing to make amends where we have done harm, provided that we do not bring about still more harm in so doing. In other words, we treat sex as we would any other problem. In meditation, we ask God what we should do about each specific matter. The right answer will come, if we want it. _____ alone can judge our sex situation."
(#6 on Inventory Guide) (Prayer) (69)

43. "Suppose we fall short of the chosen ideal and stumble? Does this mean we are going to get drunk? Some people tell us so. But this is only a half-truth. It depends on us and on our _____. If we are sorry for what we have done, and have the honest desire to let God take us to better things, we believe we will be forgiven and will have learned our lesson. If we are not sorry, and our _____ continues to _____ others, we are quite sure to _____. We are not _____. These are facts out of our experience." (70)

44. "To sum up about sex: We earnestly pray for the right ideal, for guidance in each questionable situation, for _____ , and for the strength to do the right thing. If sex is very troublesome, we throw ourselves the harder into helping others. We think of their needs and work for them. This takes us out of ourselves. It quiets the imperious urge, when to yield would mean heartache."
(Prayer) (70)

45. "If we have been thorough about our personal inventory, we have written down a lot. We have listed and _____ our resentments. We have begun to comprehend their futility and their fatality. We have commenced to see their terrible destructiveness. We have begun to learn tolerance, patience and good will toward all men, even our enemies, for we look on them as sick people. We have listed the people we have hurt by our conduct, and are willing to straighten out the past if we can." (70)

46. "In this book you read again and again that faith did for us what we could not do for ourselves. We hope you are convinced now that God can remove whatever self-will has blocked you off from Him. If you have already made a decision, and an inventory of your _____ handicaps, you have made a good beginning. That being so you have swallowed and digested some big chunks of truth about yourself." (71)

47. WHAT IS TO BE THE WATCHWORD WHEN TAKING AN INVENTORY?
_____ (12x12, 54)

48. WHAT WILL BE THE FIRST TANGIBLE EVIDENCE OF YOUR COMPLETE WILLINGNESS TO MOVE FORWARD? _____ (12x12, 54)

REVIEW THESE QUESTIONS FOR SEX, BEFORE YOU START.
1. When, and how, and in just what instances did my selfish pursuit of the sex relation damage other people and me?
2. What people were hurt, and how badly?
3. Did I spoil my marriage and injure my children?
4. Did I jeopardize my standing in the community?
5. Just how did I react to these situations at the time?
6. Did I burn with a guilt that nothing could extinguish?
7. Did I insist that I was the pursued and not the pursuer, and thus absolve myself?
8. How have I reacted to frustration in sexual matters?
9. When denied, did I become vengeful or depressed?
10. Did I take it out on other people?
11. If there was rejection or coldness at home, did I use this as a reason for promiscuity? (12x12, 50, 51)

INVENTORY FOR SEX CONDUCT

1. We listed all people we harmed. (Start with today's memories and work backward from there. Complete Column 1 from top to bottom. Do nothing on Columns 2, 3, 4, or 5 and instruction # 6 until Column 1 is complete.)

2. We asked ourselves what we did? (Complete Column 2 from top to bottom. Do nothing on Columns 3, 4, or 5 and instruction # 6 until Column 2 is complete.)

3. Which part of self caused the harm. Was it our self-esteem, our security, our ambitions, our personal or sex relations which caused the harm? (Complete each column within Column 3 going from top to bottom. Starting with the Self-Esteem and finishing with the Sexual Ambitions Column. Do nothing on Columns 4, or 5 and instruction # 6 until Column 3 is complete.)

4. Referring to our list again. Putting out of our minds the wrongs others had done, we resolutely looked for our own mistakes. Where had we been selfish, dishonest, self-seeking and frightened and inconsiderate? (Asking ourselves the above questions we complete each column within Column 4. Do nothing on Column 5 or instruction # 6 until Column 4 is complete.)

5. The Inventory was ours, not the others man's. When we saw our faults we listed them. By now we have probably arrived at the following conclusion: that our Character Defects represent Instincts gone astray. Look for the Nature or the Cause, which is one or more of the Instincts causing the condition. (Looking for the affected Instincts, we complete each column within Column 5. Do nothing about instruction # 6 until Column 5 is complete.)

6. Reading from left to right we now see the harm (Column 1), what we did (Column 2), the part of self that caused the harm (Column 3), the symptom of the Nature (Column 4), and the Exact Nature or Cause of the Harm and Behavior; which are the INSTINCTS (Column 5) that blocked us off from God's will.

COLUMN 1	COLUMN 2	COLUMN 3 — WHICH PART OF SELF IS AFFECTED?									COLUMN 4 — What is the Symptom of the Nature of our wrongs, faults, mistakes, defect, shortcomings.				COLUMN 5 — What is the exact NATURE (Instincts) of our defects, or the CAUSE of behavior		
		Social Instinct			Security Instinct			Sex Instinct							Social	Security	Sexual
Whom Did I Hurt?	What Did I Do?	Self-Esteem	Personal Relationships	Ambitions	Material	Emotional	Ambitions	Hidden Sex Relations	Acceptable Sex Relations	Ambitions	Selfish	Dishonest	Self-Seeking Frightened	Inconsiderate			
1														Prayer	Prayer
2															
3														Prayer
4														
5														
6														
7														
8														
9														
10														
11														
12														

NOTES

1. "If we have swept the searchlight of Step Four back and forth over our careers, and it has revealed in stark relief those experiences we'd rather not remember, if we have come to know how wrong _____ and _____ have hurt us and others, then the need to quit living by ourselves with those tormenting ghosts of yesterday gets more urgent than ever. We have to _____ to somebody about them.   (12x12, 55)

2. "Most of us would declare that without a fearless admission of our _____ to another human being we could not stay sober. It seems plain that the grace of _____ will not enter to expel our destructive obsessions until we are willing to try this."   (12x12, 56, 57)

3. WHAT MAY WE RECEIVE FROM STEP FIVE? _____ _____ (12x12, 57)

4. STEP FIVE IS THE BEGINNING OF WHAT? _____ _____ (12x12, 57)

5. HOW ARE WE TO BE FORGIVEN? _____ _____ (12x12, 57, 58)

6. DEFINE HUMILITY AND WHAT IS THE FIRST PRACTICAL MOVE TOWARD IT?
    A _____
    _____
    _____
    B _____ (12x12, 58)

7. "Only by discussing ourselves, holding back nothing, only by being willing to take _____ and accept _____ could we set foot on the road to straight _____ , solid honesty, and genuine humility."   (12x12, 59)

8. TRYING TO DEAL WITH GOD ALONE CAN CAUSE TWO DIFFICULTIES, LIST THEM: A _____
    _____
    _____
    _____
    B _____
    _____
    _____
    _____ (12x12, 59, 60)

9. "No one ought to say the A.A. program requires no _____ ; here is one place you may require all you've got."   (12x12, 61)

10. WHAT WILL END ISOLATION AND GIVE A FEELING OF BEING AT ONE WITH GOD AND MAN? _____
    _____ (12x12, 62)

11. WE ADMIT TO GOD, TO OURSELVES, AND TO ANOTHER HUMAN BEING THE _____ _____ OF OUR _____. (72)

12. "If we skip this _____ step, we may not overcome drinking. Time after time newcomers have tried to keep to themselves certain _____ about their lives." (72)

13. "Trying to avoid this humbling experience, they have turned to easier methods. Almost invariably they got _____." (72, 73)

14. THE PERSON WE TAKE THE FIFTH STEP WITH SHOULD BE A _____ - _____ AND _____ FRIEND. (74)

15. LIST THE NINE PROMISES WE MAY RECEIVE FROM THE FIFTH STEP.
    A _____
    B _____
    C _____
    _____
    D _____
    E _____
    _____
    F _____
    _____
    G _____
    _____
    H _____
    I _____
    _____
    _____ (75)

16. OUR SPIRITUAL EXPERIENCE MAY START WHEN? _____
    _____ (75)

17. RETURNING HOME AFTER THE FIFTH STEP, WHAT ARE WE TO DO?
    A _____
    _____
    B _____
    _____
    C _____
    _____
    _____
    D _____
    _____
    E _____
    _____
    F _____
    _____
    G _____
    _____ (75)

18. IF WE CAN ANSWER YES TO ALL OF THE ABOVE, WHAT ARE WE TO DO NEXT? _____ (76)

NOTES

NOTES

55

Chapter 6   INTO ACTION   Step #6
(76)   (12x12, 63 - 69)

1. WHAT IS INDISPENSABLE? _____ (76)

2. DEFINE WILLINGNESS: _____ (76)

3. "Are we now ready to let God remove from us all the things which we have
_____ are _____ ?" (76)

4. IF WE STILL CLING TO SOME OF OUR DEFECTS, WHAT ARE WE TO DO?
_____ (76)

5. IF WE HAVE COME A LONG WAY SPIRITUALLY, WHAT HAVE WE
REPEATEDLY DONE? _____
_____
_____
WHAT ARE WE ENTITLED TO BE CALLED? _____
_____
_____ (12x12, 63)

6. WHAT DO I NEED TO DO, SO GOD WILL REMOVE MY OBSESSION TO
DRINK? A _____
B _____
_____ (12x12, 63)

7. "They work against their own deepest instinct. As they are _____
by the terrific beating administered by _____ , the
grace of God can enter them and _____ obsession." (12x12, 64)

8. "Indeed, God made him that way. He did not _____ man to
destroy himself by _____ , but He did give man _____
to help him to stay alive." (12x12, 64)

9. "Since most of us are born with an abundance of natural _____ ,
it isn't strange that we often let these far exceed their intended purpose. When
they drive us _____ , or we _____
demand that they supply us with more satisfactions or pleasures than are
possible or due us, that is the point at which we depart from the degree of
perfection that God wishes for us here on earth. That is the measure of our
_____ _____ , or if you wish, of our sins." (12x12, 65)

10. WHAT IS THE BEST POSSIBLE ATTITUDE ONE CAN TAKE IN ORDER TO
MAKE A BEGINNING ON THIS LIFETIME JOB? _____
_____ (12x12, 65)

11. WHAT IS THE STICKING POINT? _____
_____ (12x12, 66)

12. "This I will *never* give up!" Such is the power of our _____
to overreach themselves. No matter how far we have progressed, desires will
always be found which oppose the _____ _____ _____." (12x12, 66)

13. LIST THE SEVEN DEADLY SINS: A_____ B_____
    C_____ D_____ E_____
    F_____ G_____ (12x12, 66, 67)

14. WE MUST RECOGNIZE THAT WE EXULT IN WHAT? _____
    _____ (12x12, 66)

15. DEFINE SLOTH: _____
    _____ (12x12, 67)

16. "Therefore, it seems plain that few of us can quickly or easily become ready to
    aim at spiritual and moral _____ ; we want to settle for only
    as much perfection as will get us _____ in life, according, of course, to our
    various and sundry ideas of what will get us by. So the difference between "the
    boys and the men" is the difference between striving for a _____ - determined
    objective and for the _____ objective which is of God."   (12x12, 68)

17. WHAT ARE THE MEASURING STICKS? WHAT DO WE MEASURE WITH
    THEM?   A_____
    B_____ (12x12, 68)

18. "We shall need to raise our eyes toward _____ , and be ready
    to walk in that _____." (12x12, 68)

19. THE MOMENT WE SAY "NO NEVER," WHAT HAPPENS?
    _____
    _____
    EXPLAIN: _____
    _____
    _____
    _____
    _____ (12x12, 69)

20. WE KNOW THAT WE ACT ON THE WORLD OUT OF OUR INSTINCTS AND
    THAT THEY SOMETIMES DRIVE US BLINDLY OR WE WILLFULLY DEMAND
    THAT THEY SUPPLY US WITH MORE SATISFACTION OR PLEASURE THAN
    ARE POSSIBLE OR DUE US. THIS IS OUR DISTANCE FROM GOD AND THE
    MEASURE OF OUR DEFECTS OF CHARACTER OR SIN. WE REDUCE
    THESE DEMANDS BY FORCING OURSELVES **NOT** TO DO WHAT WE **WANT**
    TO DO. THIS IS THE ESSENCE OF STEP SIX. HOW DO WE ACCOMPLISH
    THIS? WE MUST BE WILLING TO DO STEP SEVEN.
    AGREE or DISAGREE (12x12, 68, 69, 76)

NOTES

NOTES

Chapter 6   INTO ACTION   Step #7
(76)   (12x12, 70 - 76)

1. WHAT IS THE SEVENTH STEP PRAYER? _____
    _____
    _____
    _____
    _____
    _____
    _____
    _____
    _____ (76)

2. FAITH WITHOUT WORKS IS DEAD. WE NEED MORE OF WHAT TO BUILD
    FAITH? _____ (76)

3. "Indeed, the attainment of greater _____ is the foundation
    principle of each of A.A.'s Twelve Steps."   (12x12, 70)

4. WHAT IS THE DAILY BASIS OF LIVING? _____
    _____
    _____ (12x12, 72)

5. WHAT IS THE BASIC INGREDIENT OF ALL HUMILITY? _____
    _____ (12x12, 72)

6. "Still goaded by sheer necessity, we reluctantly come to grips with those
    serious _____ _____ that made problem drinkers
    of us in the first place, flaws which _____ be dealt with to prevent a
    retreat into alcoholism once again."   (12x12, 73)

7. "Where humility had formerly stood for a forced feeding on humble pie, it now
    begins to mean the nourishing ingredient which can give us _____
    _____."   (12x12, 74)

8. "In every case, pain had been the price of admission into a new _____.
    But this admission price had purchased more than we expected. It brought a
    measure of _____ , which we soon discovered to be a healer of
    pain. We began to fear pain less and desire humility more than ever." (12x12, 75)

9. IN THE PROCESS OF LEARNING ABOUT HUMILITY, WHAT CAN HAPPEN?
    _____
    _____
    _____
    _____ (12x12, 75)

10. "We saw we needn't always be _____ and
    _____ into humility. It could come quite as much from
    our _____ reaching for it as it could from unremitting
    suffering. A great _____ _____ in our lives came
    when we sought for humility as something we really wanted, rather than as
    something we *must* have."   (12x12, 75)

11. "We have seen that _____ _____ based upon shortsighted or unworthy desires are the obstacles that block our path toward these objectives. We now clearly see that we have been making _____ _____ upon ourselves, upon others, and upon God." (12x12, 76)

12. IDENTIFY THE CHIEF ACTIVATOR OF OUR DEFECTS.

    _____
    _____
    EXPLAIN: _____
    _____
    _____
    _____ (12x12, 76)

13. "Living upon a basis of unsatisfied _____ , we were in a state of continual _____ and _____. Therefore, no peace was to be had unless we could find a means of _____ these demands." (12x12, 76)

14. "The Seventh Step is where we make the change in our _____ which permits us, with _____ as our guide, to move out from ourselves toward others and toward God. The whole emphasis of Step Seven is on _____." (12x12, 76)

15. OUR ACTIONS ARE ATTEMPTS TO FILL OUR INSTINCTS. WE MUST FIND A WAY OF **REDUCING** EXCESS **DEMANDS** ON OUR INSTINCTS. FIRST WE MUST KNOW THE CAUSES AND CONDITIONS (Step Four), WHICH WILL ALLOW FOR OTHER CHOICES IN THE ACTIONS WE USE TO SATISFY OUR INSTINCTS. AGREE or DISAGREE (12x12, 76)

16. STEP SIX (FORCING OURSELVES **NOT** TO DO WHAT WE **WANT** TO DO), HELPS US TO IDENTIFY THE ACTIONS WE WANT TO REFRAIN FROM TAKING. WE CAN NOW DO STEP SEVEN - - - - FORCING OURSELVES **TO DO** WHAT WE **DON'T WANT** TO DO. WITH TIME AND PRACTICE WE WILL COME TO WANT TO DO WHAT WE FORMERLY RESISTED DOING. AGREE or DISAGREE (12x12, 76)

NOTES

NOTES

1. WHEN DID WE MAKE OUR EIGHTH STEP LIST? _____
    _____ (76)

2. "Now we go out to our fellows and _____ the
    _____ done in the _____." (76)

3. "We attempt to sweep away the _____ which has accumulated out of our
    effort to live on _____-_____ and run the _____ _____." (76)

4. "If we haven't the _____ to do this, we ask until it comes. Remember
    it was agreed at the _____ *we would go to any lengths*
    for _____ *over* _____." (76)

5. STEPS EIGHT AND NINE ARE CONCERNED WITH PERSONAL
    RELATIONSHIPS; WE NEED TO SEE THREE THINGS. LIST THEM:
    A _____
    _____
    _____
    _____
    _____
    B _____
    _____
    _____
    _____
    _____
    C _____
    _____
    _____
    _____
    _____ (12x12, 77)

6. "But if a willing start is made, then the great advantages of doing this will so
    quickly reveal themselves that the _____ will be
    _____ as one obstacle after another melts away.
    These obstacles, however, are very real. The first, and one of the most
    difficult, has to do with _____. The moment we ponder a
    twisted or broken relationship with another person, our emotions go on the
    _____. To escape looking at the _____
    we have done another, we _____ _____ on
    the wrong he has done us. This is especially true if he has, in fact, behaved
    badly at all. Triumphantly we seize upon _____ misbehavior as the
    perfect _____ for _____ or
    _____ our own." (12x12, 77,78)

7. "There were cases, too, where we had damaged others who were still happily
    _____ of being hurt. Why, we cried, shouldn't bygones be
    bygones? Why do we have to think of these people at all? These were some
    of the ways in which _____ conspired with _____ to
    hinder our making a list of _____ the people we had harmed. (12x12, 79)

8. EXPLAIN PURPOSEFUL FORGETTING. _____

_____

_____

_____

_____

HOW DO YOU CHANGE THIS ATTITUDE?_____

_____

_____ (12x12, 79)

9. "In many instances we shall find that though the harm done others has not been _____ , the _____ harm we have done ourselves has. Very deep, sometimes quite _____ , damaging emotional conflicts persist below the level of _____. At the time of these occurrences, they may actually have given our _____ violent twists which have since discolored our _____ and altered our _____ for the worse." (12x12, 79, 80)

10. WHAT HAS BEEN THE CAUSE OF OUR ALCOHOLISM?

_____

_____

EXPLAIN: _____

_____

_____

_____

_____

_____ (12x12, 80)

11. "To define the word 'harm' in a practical way, we might call it the result of _____ in collision, which cause _____ , _____ , _____ , or _____ damage to people. If our _____ are consistently bad, we arouse anger in others. If we _____ or _____ , we deprive others not only of their worldly goods, but of their emotional security and peace of mind. We really issue them an invitation to become contemptuous and vengeful. If our _____ conduct is selfish, we may excite jealousy, misery, and a strong desire to retaliate in kind." (12x12, 80)

12. "Having carefully surveyed this whole area of _____ relations, and having decided exactly what _____ traits in us injured and disturbed others, we can now commence to ransack _____ for the people to whom we have given offense." (12x12, 81)

13. TO WHAT COURSE ARE WE TO HOLD OURSELVES?

A _____

B _____

C _____

D _____

E _____ (12x12, 81, 82)

14. WHAT IS ONE OF THE PROMISES THAT COMES OUT OF STEP EIGHT?

_____

_____ (12x12, 82)

NOTES

NOTES

Chapter 6   INTO ACTION   Step #9
(76 - 84)   (12x12, 83 - 87)

1. "To some people we need not, and probably should not emphasize the spiritual feature on our first approach. We might prejudice them. At the moment we are trying to put our lives in order. But this is not an end in itself."
GOD PUT US UNDER HIS CARE AND DIRECTION: WHAT IS OUR REAL PURPOSE? _____

_____
EXPLAIN HOW WE FILL IT? _____
_____
_____
_____ (76, 77)

2. "But our man is sure to be impressed with a _____ desire to set right the wrong. He is going to be more interested in a _____ of good will than in our _____ of spiritual discoveries."   (77)

3. IF WE ARE GOING TO ANNOUNCE OUR CONVICTIONS, WE SHOULD DO IT WITH _____ AND _____ _____. (77)

4. "Under no condition do we _____ such a person or argue. Simply we tell him that we will never get over drinking until we have done our utmost to straighten out the _____. We are there to sweep off our side of the street, realizing that nothing worth while can be accomplished until we do so, never trying to tell him what he should do. His faults are _____ discussed. We stick to _____ own. If our manner is calm, frank, and open, we will be gratified with the result."   (77, 78)

5. WHY DO WE NEED TO LOSE OUR FEAR OF OUR CREDITORS?
_____
_____ (78)

6. WHAT ARE THE TWO GUIDING PRINCIPLES FOR STEP NINE?
A _____
_____
B _____
_____
_____ (79)

7. "Before taking drastic action which might implicate other people we secure their _____. If we have obtained permission, have consulted with _____ , asked _____ to help and the drastic step is indicated we must not shrink."   (80)

8. "The chances are that we have _____ troubles. Perhaps we are mixed up with women in a fashion we wouldn't care to have advertised. We doubt if, in this respect, _____ are _____ much worse than other people."   (80, 81)

9. WHAT ARE THE TWO REQUIREMENTS FOR MEANINGFUL AMENDS?
A _____
B _____ (81)

10. "Sometimes we hear an alcoholic say that the only thing he needs to do is to keep _____. Certainly he must keep sober, for there will be no home if he doesn't. But he is yet a long way from making _____ to the wife or parents whom for years he has so shockingly treated."   (82)

11. "We feel a man is _____ when he says that sobriety is enough."   (82)

12. "The spiritual life is not a theory." WHAT MUST WE DO? _____

    _____

    EXPLAIN HOW THIS ACCOMPLISHED: _____

    _____

    _____

    _____ (83)

13. WE MUST CONSIDER WHAT FOUR IDEAS IF WE INTEND NOT TO BE SERVILE OR SCRAPING, BUT STAND ON OUR FEET. A_____

    B_____ C_____ D_____

    "As _____ people we stand on our feet; we don't crawl before anyone." (83)

14. "If we are _____ about this phase of our development, we will _____ before we are half way through."   (83)

15. HOW MANY PROMISES ARE ON PAGE 83 AND THE TOP OF 84? _____
    THINK ABOUT THEIR SIGNIFICANCE.   (83, 84)

16. "They will always materialize if we _____ for _____." (84)

17. WHAT QUALITIES DO WE NEED FOR STEP NINE?

    A_____ B_____

    C_____ D_____. (12x12, 83)

18. INTO WHAT FOUR CLASSES DO WE DIVIDE OUR AMENDS LIST?

    A_____

    _____

    B_____

    _____

    C_____

    _____

    D_____

    _____ (12x12, 83)

19. "Good judgment will suggest that we ought to take our time. While we may be quite _____ to reveal the very worst, we must be sure to remember that we cannot buy our _____ peace of _____ at the expense of _____."   (12x12, 84)

20. "After taking this preliminary trial at making amends, we may enjoy such a sense of relief that we conclude our task is _____. We will want to rest on our _____. The temptation to _____ the more humiliating and dreaded meetings that still remain may be great."
    DEFINE LAURELS: _____

    _____

    _____ (12x12, 85)

21. WILL THERE BE TIMES WHEN WE WON'T REVEAL EVERYTHING TO
    SOMEONE WE OWE AMENDS? _____
    EXPLAIN: _____
    _____
    _____ (12x12, 85)

22. "There can only be _____ consideration which should qualify our
    desire for a _____ disclosure of the damage we have
    done. That will arise in the occasional situation where to make a _____
    revelation would seriously harm the one to whom we are making amends.
    Or--quite as important--other people."   (12x12, 86)

23. FROM WHOM DO WE ASK FOR GUIDANCE ON AMENDS?
    A_____ B_____ C_____
    WHAT MUST WE RESOLVE TO DO NEXT? _____
    _____
    _____ (12x12, 86)

24. "But all of them do require a _____ _____
    to make amends as _____ and as _____ as
    may be possible in a given set of conditions."   (12x12, 87)

25. "Above all, we should try to be absolutely sure that we are not delaying
    because we are _____."   (12x12, 87)

26. WHAT TWO IDEAS MAKE UP THE SPIRIT OF STEP NINE?
    A_____
    _____
    _____
    B_____
    _____
    _____ (12x12, 87)

NOTES

1. "This thought brings us to *Step Ten,* which suggests we continue to take
    _____ inventory and continue to set _____ any new
    mistakes as we go along. We vigorously commenced this way of living as we
    cleaned up the _____."
    TO TAKE AN EFFECTIVE PERSONAL INVENTORY WE MUST:
    A. KNOW WHAT WE ARE POWERLESS OVER (Step One);
    B. KNOW THE EXISTENCE OF THE ANSWER OR SOLUTION
        TO OUR PROBLEM (Step Two), AND
    C. MAKE A DECISION ON THOSE POINTS (Step Three).
    THIS FOUNDATION WILL ALLOW US TO ACT ON THE DECISION AND DO
    AN INVENTORY (Step Four).   AGREE or DISAGREE   (84)

    IF WE WANT TO VIGOROUSLY CLEAR UP THE PAST WE MUST HAVE AN
    AMENDS LIST AND ACT ON THAT LIST (Steps Eight and Nine).
                                        AGREE or DISAGREE   (84)

2. WHAT HAVE WE ENTERED? _____
    _____
    WHAT IS OUR NEXT FUNCTION? _____
    _____
    EXPLAIN HOW: _____
    _____
    _____
    _____
    _____
    _____
    _____
    _____ (84)

3. "This is not an overnight matter. It should continue for our _____.
    Continue to watch for selfishness, dishonesty, _____ , and fear."
    BEING WATCHFUL REQUIRES A PERSONAL INVENTORY:
    A. KNOW WHAT WE ARE POWERLESS OVER (Step One):
    B. KNOW THE EXISTENCE OF THE ANSWER OR SOLUTION
        TO OUR PROBLEM (Step Two), AND
    C. MAKE A DECISION ON THOSE POINTS (Step Three).
    THIS FOUNDATION WILL ALLOW US TO ACT ON THE DECISION AND DO
    AN INVENTORY (Step Four).   AGREE or DISAGREE   (84)

4. "When these crop up, we ask _____ at once to remove them."
    OUR INVENTORY DISCLOSES DEFECTS WHICH NEED ATTENTION. THIS
    CAN BE ACCOMPLISHED BY DOING STEP #6 (FORCING OURSELVES **NOT**
    TO DO **WHAT** WE WANT TO DO), AND STEP #7 (FORCING OURSELVES
    TO DO WHAT WE **DON'T WANT** TO DO).   AGREE or DISAGREE   (84)

5. "We _____ them with someone immediately and make
    _____ quickly if we have harmed anyone."
    HAVING WRITTEN OUR INVENTORY, WE NOW DISCUSS IT WITH
    SOMEONE (Step Five). WE WRITE AN AMENDS LIST (Step Eight), AND
    MAKE DIRECT AMENDS (Step Nine).   AGREE or DISAGREE   (84)

6. "Then we resolutely turn our _____ to someone we can help. Love and tolerance of others is our code."
THE RESULTS OF EFFECTIVELY WORKING STEPS TEN AND ELEVEN IS THE TURNING OF OUR THOUGHTS TO GOD AND OTHERS.

                                        AGREE or DISAGREE   (84)

QUESTIONS ONE THROUGH SIX DEMONSTRATE OUR FIRST NINE STEPS ARE MAINTAINED IN STEP TEN AND ADDRESS OUR THINKING. STEP TEN ALSO CONTAINS THE WILLINGNESS TO DO STEP ELEVEN.

                                        AGREE or DISAGREE   (84)

7. ON PAGES 83, 84 AND 85 ARE A NUMBER OF PROMISES, HOW MANY ARE THERE? _____ CONSIDER THEIR CONTEXT.   (83, 84, 85)

8. "It is easy to let up on the spiritual program of _____ and rest on our _____. We are headed for trouble if we do, for alcohol is a subtle foe. We are not cured of alcoholism."   (85)

9. "What we really have is a daily reprieve contingent on the maintenance of our spiritual condition. Every day is a day when we must carry the vision of God's will into all of our activities. 'How can I best serve Thee--Thy will (not mine) be done.' "   HOW IS THIS ACCOMPLISHED?

_____
_____ (85)

10. WHAT ARE THE THOUGHTS THAT MUST GO WITH US?

_____
_____
_____

WHAT IS ANOTHER NAME FOR OUR WILL?_____
_____ (85)

11. WHAT IS THE PROPER USE OF THE WILL? _____
_____
_____ (85)

12. WHAT IS THE VITAL SIXTH SENSE? _____
_____ WHAT ARE ITS THREE COMPONENTS?
A _____
B _____
C _____ (85)

13. WE WILL SENSE THE FLOW OF HIS SPIRIT INTO US, IF WE HAVE DONE WHAT? _____
_____
_____
_____ (85)

14. WHAT IS REQUIRED TO KEEP AND MAINTAIN THE VITAL SIXTH SENSE?

_____
_____
_____
_____ (85)

15. "As we work the first nine Steps, we prepare ourselves for the adventure of a new life. But when we approach Step Ten we commence to put our A.A. way of _____ to practical use, day by day, in fair weather or foul. Then comes the acid test; can we stay _____ , keep in _____ balance, and live to good purpose under _____ conditions?" APPLYING WHAT WE HAVE LEARNED, WE CAN SAY THAT THE FIRST NINE STEPS BROUGHT US INTO THE A.A. WAY OF LIVING.

    AGREE or DISAGREE (12x12, 88)

16. "For the wise have always known that no one can make much of his life until _____ - _____ becomes a regular habit, until he is able to _____ and _____ what he finds, and until he patiently and persistently tries to _____ what is wrong." (12x12, 88)

17. WHAT IS THE CAUSE OF AN EMOTIONAL HANGOVER? _____
    _____
    _____
    HOW DO WE TAKE CARE OF IT? _____
    _____ (12x12, 88)

18. WHAT ARE THE THREE TYPES OF INVENTORIES? EXPLAIN EACH:
    A _____
    _____
    _____
    B _____
    _____
    _____
    C _____
    _____
    _____ (12x12, 89)

19. DEFINE SPIRITUAL AXIOM: _____
    _____
    _____ (12x12, 90)

20. "The _____ inventory is aimed at our daily ups and downs, especially those where people or new events throw us off _____ and tempt us to make mistakes.
        In all these situations we need _____ - _____ , honest _____ of what is involved, a _____ to _____ when the fault is _____ , and an equal willingness to _____ when the fault is elsewhere. We need not be discouraged when we fall into the error of our old ways, for these disciplines are not easy." (12x12, 91)

21. WHAT IS OUR FIRST OBJECTIVE TOWARD IMPROVING OUR ANGER OR TEMPER? _____
    EXPLAIN HOW TO ACHIEVE THIS OBJECTIVE: _____
    _____
    _____
    _____
    _____ (12x12, 91)

22. WHAT CAN WE DO TO INSURE AGAINST "BIG-SHOT-ISM"? _____
_____
_____
_____ (12x12, 92)

23. "Finally, we begin to see that all people, including ourselves, are to some extent
_____ ill as well as frequently _____ , and
then we approach true _____ and see what real _____
for our fellows actually means. It will become more and more evident as we go
forward that it is pointless to become _____ , or to get hurt by people
who, like us, are suffering from the pains of _____ _____." (12x12, 92)

24. HOW DO WE COPE WITH OR TREAT PEOPLE WE DISLIKE? _____
_____
_____
_____ (12x12, 93)

25. IT'S A POOR DAY WHEN WE HAVEN'T DONE WHAT? _____
_____ (12x12, 93)

26. WHAT HAD TO COME BEFORE SOBRIETY; BEFORE SERENITY?
A _____
B _____ (12x12, 94)

27. WHAT IS OUR ANCIENT ENEMY? _____
EXPLAIN: _____
_____
_____
_____
_____ (12x12, 94)

28. WHY DO WE SOMETIMES HURT THE ONES WE LOVE?
_____
_____
_____ (12x12, 94)

29. "We were depressed and complained we felt bad, when in fact we were mainly
asking for _____ and _____. This odd trait
of _____ and _____ , this perverse wish to hide a
bad _____ underneath a _____ one, permeates human affairs
from top to bottom. This subtle and elusive kind of self-righteousness can
underlie the smallest _____ or _____." (12x12, 94, 95)

30. WHAT IS THE ESSENCE OF CHARACTER BUILDING? _____
_____
_____
_____
_____ (12x12, 95)

31. "Having so considered our day, not _____ to take due note of things
_____ _____ , and having searched our hearts with neither fear
nor favor, we can truly thank _____ for the blessings we have received
and sleep in good _____." (12x12, 95)

STEP TEN

Continued to take personal inventory and when we were wrong promptly admitted it.

ALCOHOLICS ANONYMOUS Pg. 84

This thought brings us to *Step Ten,* which suggests we continue to take **personal inventory** and continue to set right any new **mistakes** as we go along. We vigorously commenced this way of living as we cleaned up the past. We have entered the world of the Spirit. Our next function is to grow in understanding and effectiveness. This is not an overnight matter. It should continue for our lifetime. Continue to **watch** for selfishness, dishonesty, resentment, and fear. When these crop up, we ask **God** at once to remove them. We **discuss** them with someone immediately and make **amends** quickly if we have harmed anyone. Then we resolutely turn our **thoughts** to someone we can help. Love and tolerance of others is our code.

And we have ceased fighting anything or anyone - even alcohol. For by this time sanity will have returned. We will seldom be interested in liquor. If tempted, we recoil from it as from a hot flame. We

ALCOHOLICS ANONYMOUS Pg. 85

react sanely and **normally**, and we will find that this has happened automatically. We will see that our new attitude toward liquor has been given us without any thought or effort on our part. It just comes! That is the miracle of it. We are not fighting it, neither are we avoiding temptation. We feel as though we had been placed in a position of neutrality-safe and protected. We have not even sworn off. Instead, the problem has been removed. It does not exist for us. We are neither cocky nor are we afraid. That is our experience. That is how we react so long as we keep in fit spiritual condition.

It is easy to let up on the spiritual **program of action** and rest on our laurels. We are headed for trouble if we do, for alcohol is a subtle foe. We are not cured of alcoholism. What we really have is a daily reprieve contingent on the maintenance of our spiritual condition. Every day is a day when we must carry the **vision of God's will** into all of our activities. "How can I best serve Thee-Thy will (not mine) be done." These are thoughts which must go with us constantly. We can exercise our will power along this line all we wish. It is the proper use of the will.

Much has already been said about receiving **strength**, **inspiration**, and **direction** from Him who has all knowledge and power. If we have carefully followed directions, we have begun to sense the flow of His Spirit into us. To some extent we have become **God-conscious**. We have begun to develop this **vital sixth sense**. But we must go further and that means more action.

Because we know our **problem** (Step One) and believe in the **solution** (Step Two), we can now make the **decision** to act on the solution (Step Three). Action on the solution requires that we take a fearless moral inventory (Step Four).

We need a list of amends to set right our mistakes (Step Eight); armed with this list we can make direct amends to those we have harmed (Step Nine).

To be watchful we must know the exact **nature** of alcoholism and the **solution** and we must **decide** to find our defects of character; thus, we have taken Steps One through Four.

When we are aware of our defects (Step Six) and ready and willing to work, we can, with God's help, do our part to have them removed (Step Seven).

After we admit our wrongs to God and ourselves, we must seek out another person in whom we can confide.

We need a list of persons we have harmed (Step Eight) and we need to make those amends (Step Nine).

When we receive strength, inspiration, and direction from God we gain the vital sixth sense -- **God Consciousness**. To go further, we need the willingness to do Step Eleven.

THE BOOK DEMONSTRATES THAT STEP 10 IS THE MAINTENANCE OF THE FIRST NINE STEPS AND THE WILLINGNESS TO DO STEP 11. IF WE HAVE CAREFULLY WORKED THE FIRST NINE STEPS, WE WILL THEN MAINTAIN THEM IN STEP 10 AS WELL AS WORK STEP 11. WE SEE THAT STEPS 10 & 11 WILL THEN GIVE US STEP 12.

NOTES

1. "*Step Eleven* suggests prayer and meditation. We shouldn't be shy on this matter of prayer. Better men than we are using it constantly. It works, if we have the proper _____ and _____ at it."   (85, 86)

2. WHAT SHOULD WE DO BEFORE WE RETIRE AT NIGHT? _____
    _____ (86)

3. OUR DAY CONSISTS OF POSITIVE AND NEGATIVE; WE NEED TO REVIEW BOTH.   TRUE or FALSE (86)

4. WHAT ARE WE TO DO AFTER OUR REVIEW? _____
    _____
    _____

    EXPLAIN WHAT WE MAY RECEIVE: _____
    _____
    _____ (86)

5. WE ASK GOD FOR DIRECTION; WHAT TWO AREAS OF SELF DO WE ASK GOD TO DIRECT?   A _____ B _____ (86, 87)

6. "...GOD gave us _____ to _____." (86)

7. HOW WILL OUR THOUGHT-LIFE BE PLACED ON A HIGHER PLANE?
    _____
    _____ (86)

8. WHEN WE FACE INDECISION, WHAT ARE WE TO DO?
    A _____
    B _____
    C _____ (86)

9.   AFTER OUR MEDITATION, FOR WHAT SIX THINGS SHOULD WE PRAY?
    A _____
    _____
    B _____
    _____
    C _____
    _____
    D _____
    _____
    E _____
    _____
    F _____
    _____ (87)

10. DO WE ASK OUR SPOUSE OR FRIENDS TO JOIN US IN MEDITATION?
    _____ (87)

11. "There are many helpful _____ also. Suggestions about these may be obtained from one's priest, minister, or rabbi. Be _____ to see where _____ people are right. Make use of what they offer." (87)

12. WHEN WE FEEL AGITATED OR DOUBTFUL, WHAT TWO THINGS SHOULD WE DO? A _____

_____

B _____

_____ (87)

13. "We alcoholics are undisciplined. So we let God discipline us in the simple way we have just outlined."   HOW WE END OUR DAY IS IMPORTANT. A DAY PROPERLY ENDED GIVES US A QUIET REST WHICH ALLOWS US TO START THE NEXT DAY IN A CALM (or reasonable) MENTAL STATE. AFTER RISING, MEDITATION AND PRAYER ENABLE US TO CARRY OUT OUR PLAN FOR THE DAY.   AGREE or DISAGREE (88)

14. WHAT IS OUR PRINCIPAL MEANS OF CONTACT WITH GOD?

_____

_____ (12x12, 96)

15. WHO MIGHT CLING TO THE A. A. GROUP AS THEIR HIGHER POWER?
A _____
B _____ (12x12, 96)

16. "But we recoiled from meditation and prayer as obstinately as the scientist who _____ to perform a certain experiment lest it prove his pet theory _____. Of course we finally did _____ , and when unexpected results followed, we felt different; in fact we *knew* different; and so we were sold on meditation and prayer. And that, we have found, can happen to anybody who tries. It has been well said that 'almost the only scoffers at prayer are those who never _____ it enough.'" (12x12, 97)

17. "And when we turn away from meditation and prayer, we likewise deprive our_____ , our _____ , and our _____ of vitally needed support. As the body can fail its purpose for lack of nourishment, so can the _____." (12x12, 97)

18. "But when they are logically related and interwoven, the result is an unshakable foundation for life."   WHAT ARE THE THREE COMPONENTS OF THIS FOUNDATION?
A _____ B _____ C _____ (12x12, 98)

19. NOW AND THEN WE MAY BE GRANTED A GLIMPSE OF WHAT?

_____

_____ (12x12, 98)

20. "And we will be comforted and assured that our own _____ in that realm will be secure for so long as we _____ , however falteringly, to _____ and _____ the will of our own Creator." (12x12, 98)

21. MEDITATION IS OUR WAY OUT OF _____ AND INTO THE _____.   (12x12, 98)

22. READ AND CONSIDER THE ELEVENTH STEP PRAYER.   (12x12, 99)

23. IS THERE ANY DEBATE IN MEDITATION? _____ (12x12, 100)

24. "Perhaps the real trouble was our almost total inability to point _____ toward the right objectives. There's nothing the matter with _____ imagination; all sound achievement rests upon it. After all, no man can build a house until he first _____ a plan for it. Well, meditation is like that, too; it helps to envision our spiritual _____ before we try to move toward it." THE OPPOSITE OF CONSTRUCTIVE IMAGINATION MIGHT BE DESTRUCTIVE IMAGINATION, OR RESENTMENTS. THINK ABOUT EACH, AND TRY TO SEE HOW THE FIVE BODILY SENSES ARE INVOLVED IN BOTH PROCESSES. EXPLAIN: _____

_____

_____

_____

_____

_____ (12x12, 100, 101)

25. MEDITATION IS INTENSELY PRACTICAL: WHAT IS ONE OF THE FIRST FRUITS OF MEDITATION? _____ _____ (12x12, 101, 102)

26. MEDITATION OPENS OUR CHANNEL TO GOD'S GUIDANCE, AND PRAYER IS COMMONLY UNDERSTOOD AS A _____ TO _____. (12x12, 102)

27. "We ask simply that throughout the day God place in us the best _____ of His will that we can have for that day, and that we be given the grace by which we may _____ it out." EXPLAIN WHAT WE ARE ASKING GOD TO DO: _____

_____ (12x12, 102, 103)

28. AT TIMES OF EMOTIONAL DISTURBANCE, WHAT ARE WE TO DO PHYSICALLY? _____

_____

MENTALLY? _____

_____ (12x12, 102, 103)

29. EXPLAIN THE TWO-FOLD NATURE OF THE WELL-INTENTIONED UNCONSCIOUS RATIONALIZATION? A _____

_____

_____

B _____

_____

_____

_____ (12x12, 103, 104)

30. "In A.A. we have found that the actual good results of prayer are beyond _____. They are matters of _____ and _____. All those who have _____ have found _____ not ordinarily their own. They have found _____ beyond their usual capability. And they have increasingly found a peace of _____ which can stand firm in the face of difficult circumstances." (12x12, 104)

31. TO WHAT CONVICTION CONCERNING GOD DO WE COME TO?
_____
    EXPLAIN: _____
    _____
    _____
    _____ (12x12, 105)

32. WHAT MAY BE ONE OF THE GREATEST REWARDS OF MEDITATION AND
    PRAYER? _____
    _____
    _____ (12x12, 105)

33. WHO WATCHES OVER US? _____ WHAT IS OUR PART?
    _____
    _____ (12x12, 105)

34. WE MUST LEARN TO BE PHYSICALLY STILL IF WE WANT TO BE
    COMPETENT IN MEDITATION. FIRST WE MUST TRAIN OUR **BODIES**,
    THEN OUR **MINDS**. TRAINING THE BODY TO BE STILL WILL PROBABLY
    TAKE THIRTY TO SIXTY DAYS. THIS OBJECTIVE INCLUDES **NOT**
    WORRYING ABOUT WHAT WE ARE THINKING. AFTER THIS HAS BEEN
    ACCOMPLISHED, WE CAN PRACTICE CALMING THE MIND. AS THE BOOK,
    TWELVE STEPS AND TWELVE TRADITIONS SUPPORTS, WE SHOULD
    THINK ABOUT A SPIRITUAL PRINCIPLE OR PART OF THE ELEVENTH
    STEP PRAYER; THIS WILL MOVE US DEEPER INTO MEDITATION. WITH
    THIS DISCIPLINE IN PLACE, WE CAN BEGIN TO PUT MEDITATION TO
    PRACTICAL USE, ONE DAY AT A TIME.   AGREE or DISAGREE

STEP ELEVEN

Sought through prayer and meditation to improve our conscious contact with God *as we understood Him,* praying only for knowledge of His will for us and the power to carry that out.

ALCOHOLICS ANONYMOUS Pg. 86
When we retire at night, we **constructively** review our day.

Step Eleven starts at the **end** of our day when we review it in a constructive fashion. In the morning we ask God to direct our **thinking** and **actions,** but not our feelings. A.A. teaches that feelings will follow thinking and actions.

On awakening let us **think** about the twenty-four hours ahead. We consider our plans for the day. Before we begin, we ask God to direct our **thinking,** especially asking that it be divorced from self-pity, dishonest or self-seeking motives. Under these conditions we can employ our **mental faculties** with assurance, for after all God gave us **brains to use.**

We relax physically and mentally. Obviously, the recommended form of meditation cannot be pursued while performing other tasks, such as driving or sex.

In **thinking** about our day we may face indecision. We may not be able to determine which course to take. Here we ask God for inspiration, an intuitive thought or a decision. **We relax and take it easy. We don't struggle.**

When we feel upset or doubtful, we need to physically halt and calm ourselves mentally. We can then ask for the right thought or action. When **practiced,** this works.

ALCOHOLICS ANONYMOUS Pg. 87
As we go through the day **we pause, when agitated or doubtful, and ask for the right thought or action.**

ALCOHOLICS ANONYMOUS Pg. 88
We alcoholics are **undisciplined. So we let God discipline us in the simple way we have just outlined.**

We need **prayer** and **meditation** to have conscious contact with God.

TWELVE STEPS and TWELVE TRADITIONS Pg. 96
PRAYER and meditation are our principal means of conscious contact with God.

TWELVE STEPS and TWELVE TRADITIONS Pg. 97
Those of us who have come to make regular use of **prayer** would no more do without it than we would refuse air, food, or sunshine. And for the same reason. When we refuse air, light or food, the **body** suffers. And when we turn away from **meditation and prayer,** we likewise deprive our **minds,** our **emotions,** and our **intuitions** of vitally needed support.

Each of us is made of body, mind, spirit and emotions or feelings. We need conscious contact with God to support our thinking, emotions, and intuition (insight).

TWELVE STEPS and TWELVE TRADITIONS Pg. 100
Perhaps our trouble was not that we used our imagination. Perhaps the real trouble was our almost total inability to point imagination toward the right objectives. There's nothing the matter with *constructive* imagination; all sound achievement rests upon it. After all, no man can build a house until he first envisions a plan for it. Well, meditation is like that, too; it helps to **envision our spiritual objective** before we try to move toward it.

We have had inner experience with this already. The opposite of **constructive** imagination is **destructive** imagination, we call this resentment. When we are resentful we involve all five of the bodily senses. In meditation or constructive imagination we need to do the same.

TWELVE STEPS and TWELVE TRADITIONS Pg. 102
Now, what of prayer? **Prayer** is the raising of the heart and mind to God--and in this sense it includes meditation. How may we go about it? And how does it fit in with meditation? **Prayer,** as commonly understood, is a petition to God.

We first must practice physical quiet (30 - 60 days); then we can practice mental calm (30 - 60 days). With this discipline we can see, feel, touch, taste and smell the sunlit beach and sense that **we belong.**

TWELVE STEPS and TWELVE TRADITIONS Pg. 105
Perhaps one of the greatest rewards of **meditation** and prayer is the sense of *belonging* that comes to us.

1. WHAT WILL INSURE IMMUNITY FROM DRINKING? _____
    _____ _____ _____ _____ (89)

2. "So _____ ; never _____. To be helpful
    is our only _____." (89)

3. "When you discover a _____ for Alcoholics Anonymous,
    find out all you can about _____. If he does not want to stop
    _____ , don't waste _____ trying to
    _____ him."   WHY?   _____
    _____ (90)

4. IF THERE IS AN INDICATION THE NEW PROSPECT WANTS TO STOP, WHAT
    ARE WE TO DO? _____
    _____
    _____
    _____ (90)

5. IF THE NEW PROSPECT DOES NOT WANT TO SEE US, DO WE FORCE THE
    ISSUE?_____ (90)

6. "See your man alone, if possible. At first engage in _____
    _____." (91)

7. "When he sees you know all about the drinking game, commence to describe
    yourself as an _____. Tell him how baffled you were, how you
    finally learned that you were _____. Give him an account of
    the struggles you made to stop. Show him the _____
    _____ which leads to the first _____
    of a spree." (91, 92)

8. "If you are satisfied that he is a real _____ , begin to dwell on
    the hopeless_____ of the _____. Show him, from
    your own experience, how the queer _____ condition
    surrounding that first drink prevents normal functioning of the will power. Don't,
    at this stage, refer to this _____ , unless he has seen it and
    wishes to discuss it. And be careful not to brand him as an _____.
    Let him draw his own _____."   FROM OUR
    EXPERIENCE WE HELP THE NEW PROSPECT TO SEE THE EXACT
    PHYSICAL AND MENTAL NATURE OF ALCOHOLISM. THIS HELPS THEM
    UNDERSTAND AND DRAW CONCLUSIONS ABOUT THEIR CONDITION.
    AGREE or DISAGREE   (92)

9. "Continue to speak of alcoholism as an illness, a _____
    malady. Talk about the conditions of _____ and _____
    which accompany it." (92)

10. "Even though your _____ may not have entirely
    _____ his condition, he has become very curious to know
    how you got _____." (92, 93)

11. *"Tell him exactly what happened to you.* Stress the _____ feature freely. If the man be _____ or _____, make it emphatic that *he does not have to agree with your conception of God.* He can choose any conception he likes, provided it makes _____ to him. *The main thing is that he be willing to believe in a _____ greater than himself and that he live by _____ principles. "* (93)

12. "To be vital, faith _____ be accompanied by _____ _____ and unselfish, constructive _____." DRAWING ON THE BOOK, "ALCOHOLICS ANONYMOUS," EXPLAIN HOW WE ACCOMPLISH THIS.
    _____
    _____
    _____
    _____ (93)

13. WE REPRESENT NO PARTICULAR FAITH OR DENOMINATION; WE DEAL WITH WHAT? _____
    _____
    _____ (93, 94)

14. "Outline the program of _____, explaining how you made a self-appraisal, how you straightened out your _____ and why you are now endeavoring to be helpful to him." HOW THIS IS DONE? _____
    _____
    _____
    _____
    _____ (94)

15. IF YOUR ASSISTANCE ISN'T WANTED, WHO HAS BEEN HELPED?
    _____ (94)

16. "On your first visit tell him about the Fellowship of Alcoholics Anonymous. If he shows interest, lend him your copy of this _____." (94)

17. WHAT DOES THE KIT OF SPIRITUAL TOOLS CONTAIN?
    A_____ B_____
    C_____ (95)

18. "If he is _____ interested and wants to see you again, ask him to _____ _____ _____ in the interval. After doing that, he_____ _____ for himself whether he wants to go on. He should not be _____ or _____ by you, his wife, or his friends. If he is to find _____, the desire must come from within." (95)

19. SHOULD WE CHASE A PERSON WHO CANNOT OR WILL NOT WORK WITH US? _____ EXPLAIN: _____
    _____
    _____ (96)

20. CAN WE GIVE PRACTICAL ADVICE? _____ EXPLAIN: _____
    _____
    _____ (96)

21. "Never avoid these _____ , but be _____ you are doing the right thing if you assume them. Helping others is the _____ stone of your recovery. A kindly act once in a while isn't _____. You have to act the Good Samaritan _____ _____ , if need be."   IF WE DO THIS, WHAT MAY HAPPEN? _____
_____
_____
_____ (97)

22. SHOULD WE ALLOW AN ALCOHOLIC TO LIVE IN OUR HOME? _____ (97)

23. IF AN ALCOHOLIC DEPENDS UPON _____ AND NOT _____ , THEY SIMPLY WILL NOT STOP DRINKING.
                                    TRUE or FALSE   (98)

24. WHAT IDEA MUST WE BURN INTO THE CONSCIOUSNESS OF A NEW PERSON? _____
WHAT CONDITION IS NECESSARY TO ACHIEVE THIS IDEA? _____
_____ (98)

25. IF THERE HAS BEEN A DIVORCE OR SEPARATION, WHAT TWO THINGS GENERALLY MUST HAPPEN BEFORE THE COUPLE SHOULD REUNITE.
A_____
B_____ (99)

26. "Both _____ and the _____ man must walk day by day in the path of _____ _____. If you _____ , remarkable things will happen. When we look _____ , we realize that the things which came to us when we put ourselves in _____ _____ were better than anything we could have planned. Follow the _____ of a Higher Power and you will presently live in a new and wonderful world, no matter what your present _____!"
                                                        (100)

27. IF WE ARE SPIRITUALLY FIT, WHAT CAN WE DO? _____
_____
_____ (100, 101)

28. WHAT DOES IT INDICATE WHEN AN ALCOHOLIC TRIES TO AVOID THE PRESENCE OF ALCOHOL OR ALL MENTION OF IT? _____
_____
_____ (101)

29. BEFORE GOING TO AN AFFAIR WHERE DRINKING WILL OCCUR, WHAT IS THE RULE TO CONSIDER? _____
_____
_____ (101)

30. IF WE GO TO THESE AFFAIRS, WHAT SHOULD WE ASK OURSELVES?
A_____
_____
B_____
_____ (101, 102)

31. THE WORD "VICARIOUS" CAN BE DEFINED AS "FELT OR UNDERGONE AS IF ONE WERE TAKING PART IN THE EXPERIENCE OR FEELINGS OF ANOTHER." EXPLAIN THE CONTEXT OF ITS USE ON PAGES 101 AND 102 IN THE BOOK ALCOHOLICS ANONYMOUS. _____

_____

_____

_____

_____

_____ (101, 102)

32. WHAT IS OUR JOB IN HELPING OTHERS? _____

_____

WHAT MUST WE DO? _____

_____

_____ (102)

33. TO WHAT MUST WE NEVER SHOW INTOLERANCE OR HATRED AS AN INSTITUTION? _____ (103)

34. *"After all, our _____ were of our own making. Bottles were only a _____. Besides, we have stopped _____ anybody or anything. _____ _____ _____ ! "* (103)

35. IN CHAPTER SEVEN THE AUTHORS USE SIX DIFFERENT NAMES FOR THE NEW PERSON. LIST THEM.   A _____
B _____   C _____
D _____   E _____
F _____   (89, 90, 92, 95, 100, 102)

36. ALCOHOL FINALLY HELPS US TO SEE OUR PROBLEM -- OUR DISTANCE FROM GOD. THE GULF LIES BETWEEN OUR SELF-WILL AND GOD'S WILL FOR US. HIS WILL FOR US BECOMES MANIFEST, WHEN WE SUBMIT TO HIS CARE AND DIRECTION, WHICH IS THE PROGRAM OF ALCOHOLICS ANONYMOUS.   AGREE or DISAGREE

"HAVING HAD A SPIRITUAL AWAKENING AS THE RESULT OF THESE STEPS..."

37. "The joy of living is the theme of A.A.'s Twelfth Step." WHAT IS THE KEY WORD TO THIS STEP? _____ (12x12, 106)

38. HOW DO WE REACH EMOTIONAL SOBRIETY? _____

_____

_____

_____ (12x12, 106)

39. HOW DO WE HAVE A SPIRITUAL AWAKENING? _____

_____

_____

_____ (12x12, 106)

40. ON PAGES 106 AND 107 IN THE BOOK, TWELVE STEPS AND TWELVE TRADITIONS, A SPIRITUAL AWAKENING IS DESCRIBED IN FIVE SUBTLY DIFFERENT WAYS; LIST THEM.

A _____
_____
_____

B _____
_____
_____

C _____
_____
_____

D _____
_____
_____

E _____
_____
_____ (12x12, 106, 107)

41. A TRUE SPIRITUAL AWAKENING OR EXPERIENCE CHANGES THE ENTIRE PERSON. **THINKING**, **ACTIONS** AND **FEELINGS**, THE COMPLETE PERSONALITY, ARE AFFECTED. THESE THREE COMPONENTS OF THE ENTIRE PERSON ARE INTERDEPENDENT; ANY DIFFERENCE IN ONE WILL REFLECT ITSELF IN THE OTHER TWO.   AGREE or DISAGREE

42. BECOME FAMILIAR WITH THE BRIEF REVIEW OF STEPS ONE THROUGH ELEVEN ON PAGES 107 AND 109 OF "TWELVE STEPS and TWELVE TRADITIONS."   LIST SOME THOUGHTS YOU MAY HAVE ON THEM.

_____
_____
_____
_____
_____
_____ (12x12, 107, 108, 109)

43. "From great numbers of such experiences, we could predict that the _____ who still claimed that he hadn't got the '_____ _____,' and who still considered his well-loved A.A. _____ the higher power, would presently love _____ and call Him by _____." (12x12, 109)

"WE TRIED TO CARRY THIS MESSAGE TO ALCOHOLICS..."

44. AFTER THE SPIRITUAL AWAKENING, A DIFFERENT ENERGY MAY BE RELEASED. TO RECEIVE THIS ENERGY, WHAT MUST WE DO?

_____
_____
_____
_____
_____ (12x12, 109)

45. WHAT SIX THINGS ARE INCLUDED IN THE **SUBSTANCE** OF WHAT WE RECEIVE, AS WE CARRY THE A.A. MESSAGE TO THE NEXT ALCOHOLIC?

A _____

B _____

C _____

D _____

E _____

F _____

_____ (12x12, 110)

46. "For example, we may set our hearts on getting a particular person _____ up, and after doing all we can for months, we see him _____. Perhaps this will happen in a succession of cases, and we may deeply _____ as to our ability to carry A.A.'s message. Or we may encounter the reverse situation, in which we are highly _____ because we seem to have been successful. Here the_____ is to become rather _____ of these newcomers. Perhaps we try to give them _____ about their affairs which we aren't really _____ to give or ought not give at all. Then we are hurt and confused when the advice is _____ , or when it is _____ and brings still greater confusion. By a great deal of ardent Twelfth Step work we sometimes carry the message to so many alcoholics that _____ place us in a position of _____. They make us, let us say, the group's chairman. Here again we are presented with the_____ to overmanage things, and sometimes this results in _____and other consequences which are hard to_____.

But in the longer run we _____ _____ that these are only the pains of growing _____ , and nothing but _____ can come from them if we turn more and more to the _____ Twelve Steps for the _____." (12x12, 111)

"...AND TO PRACTICE THESE PRINCIPLES IN ALL OUR AFFAIRS."

47. "Can we love the _____ pattern of living as eagerly as we do the small segment of it when we try to help other _____ achieve sobriety?" (12x12, 111)

48. "Of course all A.A.'s, even the best, fall far _____ of such achievements as a consistent thing. Without necessarily _____ that first drink, we often get quite far off the beam. Our troubles sometimes begin with _____. We are sober and happy in our A.A. work. Things go well at home and office. We naturally _____ ourselves on what later proves to be a far too easy and superficial point of view. We temporarily cease to _____ because we _____ _____ that there is no need for *all* of A.A.'s Twelve Steps for us. We are doing fine on a_____ of them. Maybe we are doing fine on only _____ of them, the First Step and that part of the Twelfth where we 'carry the message.' In A.A. slang, that blissful state is known as '_____ - _____.' And it can go on for years." (12x12, 112, 113)

89

49. WHAT IS THE "PINK CLOUD" AS THAT EXPRESSION IS USED IN A.A.?
_____
_____
_____

WHAT HAPPENS WHEN IT DISSIPATES? _____
_____
_____
_____ (12x12, 113)

50. "These were problems of life which we could never face up to. Can we
_____ , with the help of _____ as we understand Him,
handle them as well and as bravely as our nonalcoholic friends often do? Can
we transform these_____ into _____ , sources of growth and
comfort to ourselves and those about us? Well, we surely have a chance if we
_____ from 'two-stepping' to 'twelve-stepping,' if we are
_____ to receive that grace of God which can sustain and
strengthen us in any _____." (12x12, 113)

51. ARE OUR BASIC TROUBLES DIFFERENT FROM ANYBODY ELSE'S?
_____
WHAT WILL TAKE US THROUGH THESE DIFFICULTIES? _____
_____
_____ (12x12, 114)

52. WHAT WILL IMPROVE OUR CHANCES FOR REALLY HAPPY AND USEFUL
LIVES? _____
_____ (12x12, 114)

53. AS WE GROW SPIRITUALLY, WHAT MUST OUR ATTITUDE TOWARD OUR
INSTINCTS UNDERGO? _____
_____
_____
_____ (12x12, 114)

54. WHAT WILL GIVE US A REAL CHANCE TO CHANGE OUR ATTITUDE?
_____
_____
_____ (12x12, 114)

55. WHAT IS THE BEST POSSIBLE SOURCE OF EMOTIONAL STABILITY?
_____
_____
_____ (12x12, 116)

56. "Permanent marriage breakups and separations, however, are _____
in A.A. Our main problem is not how we are to stay married; it is how to be more
_____ married by eliminating the severe _____
twists that have so often stemmed from alcoholism." (12x12, 117)

57. "A.A. has many _____ alcoholics who wish to marry and are in a position to do so. Some marry fellow A.A.'s. How do they come out? On the whole these marriages are very _____ ones. Their common suffering as drinkers, their common interest in A.A. and _____ things, often enhance such unions. It is only where 'boy meets girl on A.A. campus,' and love follows at first sight, that _____ may develop. The prospective partners need to be _____ A.A.'s and long enough acquainted to know that their compatibility at _____ , _____ , and _____ levels is a _____ and not wishful thinking. They need to be as _____ as _____ that no deep-lying emotional handicap in either will be likely to rise up under later pressures to cripple them. The considerations are equally true and important for the A.A.'s who marry 'outside' A.A. With clear understanding and right, grown up attitudes, very happy results do follow."

(12x12, 119, 120)

58. DOES OUR OUTLOOK ON MONEY AND MATERIAL THINGS UNDERGO A REVOLUTIONARY CHANGE? _____. MONEY WAS A SYMBOL OF WHAT? _____

_____

WHAT HAPPENED TO THESE ATTITUDES UPON ENTERING A.A.?

_____

_____

_____

_____ (12x12, 120, 121)

59. WHAT WILL RELIEVE OUR FEARS CONCERNING MONEY AND MATERIAL THINGS? _____

_____

_____ (12x12, 121)

60. DOES THE STATE OF OUR MATERIAL CONDITION MATTER TOO MUCH? _____ WHAT CONDITION IS IMPORTANT? _____

_____ (12x12, 122)

61. "The doctors weren't trying to find how different we were from one another; they sought to find whatever personality _____ , if any, this group of alcoholics had in common. They finally came up with a conclusion that shocked the A.A. members of that time. These distinguished men had the nerve to say that most of the alcoholics under investigation were still _____ , _____ sensitive, and _____ ." (12x12, 123)

62. IN THE YEARS SINCE, DID MOST A.A.'s AGREE WITH THESE DOCTORS?

_____ (12x12, 123)

63. WHAT IS THE REVERSE SIDE OF FALSE PRIDE? _____ . WHY DID WE HAVE TO BE "NUMBER ONE PEOPLE?" _____

_____

_____

_____ (12x12, 123)

64. "But today, in _____ - _____ A.A.'s these distorted drives have been_____ to something like their true purpose and direction. We no longer strive to _____ or _____ those about us in order to gain_____ - _____. We no longer seek fame and honor in order to be _____. When by devoted service to family, friends, business, or community we attract widespread affection and are sometimes singled out for posts of greater responsibility and trust, we try to be humbly grateful and exert ourselves the more in a spirit of _____ and _____. True leadership, we find, depends upon able example and not upon vain displays of power or glory." (12x12, 124)

65. EXPLAIN TRUE AMBITION: _____
_____
WHAT IS ANOTHER DEFINITION OF TRUE AMBITION? _____
_____
_____ (12x12, 124, 125) (60, 77)

66. HOW DO WE GET RIGHT WITH OURSELVES, WITH THE WORLD, AND WITH GOD? _____ (12x12, 125)

67. **UNDERSTANDING-** "a mental grasp" or "the power of the mind by which man attains truth or knowledge." **PRINCIPLE-** "a comprehensive and fundamental law, doctrine, or assumption" or "general or fundamental law." **ATTITUDES-** "a mental position with regard to a fact or state" or "a firmly held point of view or way of regarding something." Webster's Dictionary WHAT IS THE KEY TO RIGHT PRINCIPLES AND ATTITUDES?
_____
_____ (12x12, 125)

68. "Now what about the rest of the Twelfth Step? The wonderful energy it releases and the eager action by which it carries our message to the next suffering alcoholic and which finally translates the Twelve Steps into action upon all our affairs is the payoff, the magnificent reality, of Alcoholics Anonymous." (12x12, 109)

"Our real purpose is fit ourselves to be of maximum service to God and the people about us." (77)

THE SPIRITUAL AWAKENING WHICH WE RECEIVE BY LEARNING AND PRACTICING THE A.A. MESSAGE WILL FILL OUR **INSTINCTS** AND **DESIRES**. WE BEGIN TO FORM NEW PRINCIPLES AND ATTITUDES AS WE GAIN UNDERSTANDING FROM OUR TEXT BOOK AND SUPPORT FROM OUR FELLOWSHIP. WHEN WE ESTABLISH AND MAINTAIN THIS WAY OF LIFE WE BECOME RESPONSIBLE TO TRANSMIT WHAT HAS BEEN SO FREELY GIVEN. THIS IS DONE BY HELPING OTHER ALCOHOLICS RECEIVE THE MESSAGE OF A.A. THE **SPIRITUAL ENERGY RELEASED** IN US BY HELPING ANOTHER ALCOHOLIC ALLOWS US TO PRACTICE THE A.A. PRINCIPLES IN ALL OUR AFFAIRS. OUR **PURPOSE** IS TO SERVE GOD AND THE PEOPLE AROUND US. WHEN WE MAKE THE DECISION TO GO UNDER THE **CARE OF GOD**, HIS WILL FOR US IS REALIZED.
See page 118, in this Work/Study Guide. AGREE or DISAGREE (12x12, 109) (77)

STEP TWELVE

Having had a spiritual awakening as the result of these steps, we tried to carry this message to alcoholics, and to practice these principles in all our affairs.

TWELVE STEPS and TWELVE TRADITIONS Pg. 106-7
When a man or a woman has a spiritual awakening, the most important meaning of it is that he has now become able to **do**, **feel**, and **believe** that which he could not do before on his unaided strength and resources alone.

A true spiritual awakening changes us totally; therefore, we **think, act** and **feel** differently. We realize it was God's strength which accomplished this through the care of A.A.

This change in thinking, acting and feeling must be **practiced** daily to maintain it.

TWELVE STEPS and TWELVE TRADITIONS Pg. 109
So, **practicing** these Steps, **we had a spiritual awakening** about which finally there was no question.

ALCOHOLICS ANONYMOUS Pg. 89
Practical experience shows that nothing will so much insure immunity from drinking as intensive work with other alcoholics. It works when other activities fail. This is our *twelfth suggestion:* **Carry this message** to other alcoholics! You can help when no one else can. You can secure their confidence when others fail.

God has given us the ability to help others because we have had a spiritual awakening. What we share is the message of A.A., or **How To Have A Spiritual Awakening**. This keeps us from a drink as we learn to help others

We can assume these responsibilities when we diligently work the Steps, and these responsibilities protect us from drinking.

ALCOHOLICS ANONYMOUS Pg. 97
Never avoid these **responsibilities,** but be sure you are doing the right thing if you assume them. Helping others is the foundation stone of your recovery. A kindly act once in a while **isn't** enough.

The Steps are the kit of spiritual tools. We show others how these principles have worked for us.

ALCOHOLICS ANONYMOUS Pg. 95
Never talk down to an alcoholic from any moral or spiritual hilltop; simply lay out the **kit of spiritual tools** for his inspection. Show him how they worked with you. Offer him friendship and fellowship. Tell him that if he wants to get well you will do anything to help.

Spiritual work is **filling** and **releases** a wonderful energy. Carrying our message (how to have a spiritual awakening) teaches us how to practice the principles of A.A. in all our affairs.

TWELVE STEPS and TWELVE TRADITIONS Pg. 109
Now, what about the rest of the Twelfth Step? **The wonderful energy it releases** and the eager action by which it carries our **message** to the next suffering alcoholic and which finally translates the Twelve Steps into action upon **all our affairs** is the payoff, the magnificent reality, of Alcoholics Anonymous.

Constructive action is carrying the message of A.A. This means learning to put A.A. and the people in our lives ahead of self.

ALCOHOLICS ANONYMOUS Pg. 93
To be vital, faith must be accompanied by self sacrifice and unselfish, **constructive action**.

With time and perseverance, we come to understand that we need to examine whether we are practicing **all** of the Twelve Steps, whether we feel good, bad or neutral.

TWELVE STEPS and TWELVE TRADITIONS Pg. 113
We temporarily cease to grow because **we feel satisfied** that there is no need for *all* of A.A.'s Twelve Steps for us. We are doing fine on a few of them. Maybe we are doing fine on only two of them, the First Step and that part of the Twelfth where we "carry the message." In A.A. slang, that blissful state is known as "**two-stepping**." And it can go on for years.

Knowledge of the **fundamental truth** will produce the feeling, opinion, or mood; **if constructive action** takes place.

TWELVE STEPS and TWELVE TRADITIONS Pg. 125
Understanding is the key to right **principles** and **attitudes**, and right **action** is the key to good living; therefore the joy of good living is the theme of A.A.'s Twelfth Step.

NOTES

NOTES

Chapter 8   TO WIVES
(104 - 121)

1. DOES THE TEXT APPLY TO MEN AS WELL AS WOMEN? _____ (104)

2. WHAT WILL THIS CHAPTER HELP THE WIFE (or husband) OF AN ALCOHOLIC DO? _____
    _____ (104)

3. CONSIDER PAGES 104 - 107. WE MIGHT HAVE BEHAVED DIFFERENTLY HAD WE UNDERSTOOD WHAT? _____
    _____ (104 -107)

4. THERE IS ONE EXCEPTION FOR TREATING THE ALCOHOLIC AS A SICK PERSON. EXPLAIN: _____
    _____

    IF THE ALCOHOLIC IS THE EXCEPTION, WHAT MIGHT YOU DO? _____

    EXPLAIN: _____
    _____ (108)

5. THE PROBLEM IN DEALING WITH ALCOHOLICS USUALLY FALLS WITHIN ONE OF FOUR CATEGORIES. LIST SOME OF THE SYMPTOMS FOR CATEGORY ONE: _____
    _____
    _____
    _____ (108, 109)

6. LIST SOME OF THE SYMPTOMS FOR CATEGORY TWO: _____
    _____
    _____
    _____
    _____ (109)

7. THE SYMPTOMS OF CATEGORY TWO REPRESENT THE REAL ALCOHOLIC.
    TRUE or FALSE   (109)

8. LIST SOME OF THE SYMPTOMS FOR CATEGORY THREE: _____
    _____
    _____
    _____ (109, 110)

9. LIST SOME OF THE SYMPTOMS FOR CATEGORY FOUR: _____
    _____
    _____
    _____ (110)

10. THERE IS HOPE FOR ALL OF THE FOUR CATEGORIES. WITH WHICH CATEGORY OF ALCOHOLIC CAN YOU BE QUITE HOPEFUL? _____
    WHICH CATEGORY IS OFTEN DIFFICULT TO DEAL WITH? _____ (110)

11. WHAT ARE THE FOUR GENERAL PRINCIPLES TO APPLY TOWARD YOUR DRINKING SPOUSE? A _____

B _____
_____

C _____
_____

D _____
_____ (111)

12. IF YOU APPLY THE FOUR GENERAL PRINCIPLES, THEY MAY LAY THE GROUNDWORK FOR WHAT? _____
_____ (111)

13. "When a discussion does arise, you might _____ he read this _____ or at least the chapter on alcoholism. Tell him you have been worried, though perhaps needlessly. You think he ought to know the subject better, as everyone should have a clear understanding of the risk he takes if he drinks too much. Show him you have _____ in his power to stop or moderate. Say you do not want to be a wet blanket; that you only want him to take care of his health. Thus you may succeed in _____ him in alcoholism."   (111, 112)

14. IF THIS APPROACH DOES NOT WORK, WHAT ARE WE TO DO?
_____ (112)

15. "Suppose, however, that your husband fits the description of number _____ . The same principles which _____ to husband number one should be practiced. But after his next _____ , ask him if he would really like to get over drinking for good. Do _____ _____ that he do it for you or anyone else. Just would he *like* to?"
The chances are he would. Show him your copy of this _____ and tell him what you have found out about _____ . Show him that as alcoholics, the writers of the book understand. Tell him some of the interesting _____ you have _____ . If you think he will be shy of a _____ _____ , ask him to look at the chapter on alcoholism. Then perhaps he will be interested enough to continue."   (112, 113)

16. IF OUR SPOUSE IS LUKEWARM TO THIS APPROACH, WHAT ARE WE TO DO? _____ (113)

17. "If you have a number three husband, you may be in _____ . Being _____ he wants to stop, you can go to him with this _____ as joyfully as though you had struck oil. He may not share your enthusiasm, but he is practically sure to read the _____ and he may go for the program at once. If he does not, you will probably not have _____ to wait. Again, you should not _____ him. Let him decide for himself. Cheerfully see him through more sprees. Talk about his condition or this book only when he raises the issue. In some cases it may be better to let someone outside the family present the _____ . They can urge action without arousing hostility. If your husband is otherwise a _____ individual, your chances are good at this stage."   (113)

18. "You would suppose that men in the _____ classification would be quite hopeless, but that is not so. Many of Alcoholics Anonymous were like that. Everybody had given them up. Defeat seemed certain. Yet often such men had spectacular and powerful recoveries.

There are _____ . Some men have been so impaired by alcohol that they cannot stop. Sometimes there are cases where alcoholism is complicated by other _____ . A good doctor or psychiatrist can tell you whether these complications are serious. In any event, try to have your husband read this _____ . His reaction may be one of enthusiasm. If he is already committed to an institution, but can convince you and your doctor that he means business, give him a chance to try our method, unless the doctor thinks his _____ condition too abnormal or dangerous. We make this recommendation with some confidence. For years we have been working with alcoholics _____ to institutions. Since this book was first published, A.A. has _____ thousands of alcoholics from asylums and hospitals of every kind. The majority have never returned. The _____ of God goes deep!

You may have the _____ situation on your hands. Perhaps you have a husband who is at large, but who should be committed. Some men cannot or will not get over alcoholism. When they become too _____ , we think the kind thing is to lock them up, but of course a good _____ should always be consulted. The wives and children of such men suffer horribly, but not more than the men themselves." (113, 114)

19. WHAT MAY HAPPEN WHEN YOU CAREFULLY EXPLAIN THE NATURE OF YOUR SPOUSE'S ILLNESS TO CLOSE FRIENDS? _____
_____
_____
_____ (115)

20. DO WE EXPLAIN TO THE EMPLOYER OF OUR ALCOHOLIC, THAT HE OR SHE IS SICK? _____ WHO SHOULD INFORM THE EMPLOYER?
_____
_____
_____ (115)

21. WHAT IS THE PROMISE ON PAGE 116? _____
_____
_____
_____
_____ (116)

22. "We wives found that, like _____ else, we were afflicted with _____ , _____ , _____ and all the things which go to make up the _____ person; and we were not above _____ or _____ . As our husbands began to apply _____ principles in their lives, we began to see the desirability of doing so too." (116)

23. DOES THE TEXT URGE THE NONALCOHOLIC SPOUSE TO TRY THE A.A. PROGRAM AND GO TO MEETINGS WITH THE ALCOHOLIC? _____ (117)

24. WHEN WE HAVE AN HONEST DIFFERENCE OF OPINION WITH OUR SPOUSE, WE CAN DISAGREE WITH THEM. WE NEED TO BE CAREFUL OF WHAT? _____

_____

_____

_____ (117)

25. WHAT PRIVILEGE SHOULD BE APPLIED, NO MATTER WHAT THE SUBJECT, WHEN HAVING A HEATED DISCUSSION WITH YOUR SPOUSE?

_____

_____

_____

_____ (118)

26. "Your husband knows he owes you more than _____ . He wants to make good. Yet you must not expect too much. His ways of thinking and doing are the habits of years. _____ , _____ , _____ and _____ are the watchwords. Show him these things in yourself and they will be reflected back to you from him. Live and let live is the _____ . If you both show a willingness to remedy your _____ defects, there will be little need to criticize each other." (118)

27. "Another feeling we are very likely to entertain is one of _____ that love and loyalty could not _____ our husbands of alcoholism. We do not like the thought that the contents of a _____ or the work of another _____ has accomplished in a few weeks that for which we struggled for years. At such moments we forget that alcoholism is an illness over which we could not possibly have had any _____ ." (118)

28. WHAT ARE WE TO DO WHEN RESENTFUL THOUGHTS COME?

_____

_____

_____ (119)

29. "Still another difficulty is that you may become _____ of the attention he bestows on other people, especially alcoholics. You have been starving for his companionship, yet he spends long hours helping other men and their families. You feel he should now be _____ , The fact is that he should work with other people, to maintain his own _____ ." (119)

30. IF WE FEEL NEGLECTED BY THE SOBER ALCOHOLIC, WHAT CAN WE DO?

_____

_____

_____ (119)

31. WHEN THE ALCOHOLIC AND THE SPOUSE AWAKEN TO A SENSE OF RESPONSIBILITY FOR OTHERS AND WHAT THEY CAN PUT INTO LIFE INSTEAD OF WHAT THEY TAKE OUT, THEY ARE PROMISED WHAT?

A _____

B _____ (119, 120)

32. IF YOUR SPOUSE HAS A RELAPSE, WHAT MUST HE OR SHE DO?
_____
_____
_____

WHAT CAUSED THE RELAPSE? _____
_____
_____ (120)

33. AS JUSTIFICATION FOR DRINKING, THE ALCOHOLIC WILL USE WHAT?
_____
_____
_____ (120)

34. DO WE SHIELD THE ALCOHOLIC FROM THE TEMPTATIONS OF DRINKING?
_____ EXPLAIN: _____
_____
_____
_____ (120)

35. WHO REMOVES THE LIQUOR PROBLEM? _____
_____ (120)

36. WHERE DO WE PLACE ALL OUR PROBLEMS? _____
_____ (120)

37. "We realize that we have been giving you much _____ and
_____ . We may have seemed to lecture. If that is so we are
sorry, for we ourselves don't always care for people who lecture us. But what
we have related is based upon _____ , some of it
_____ . We had to learn these things the _____
way. That is why we are anxious that you _____ , and that you
avoid these unnecessary _____ . So to you out there who
may soon be with us–we say 'Good luck and God bless you!' " (121)

100

NOTES

Chapter 9 THE FAMILY AFTERWARD

(122 - 135)

1. WHAT IS THE COMMON GROUND THAT ALL FAMILY MEMBERS SHOULD MEET UPON? _____
   _____ (122)

2. WHAT HAPPENS WHEN ONE MEMBER OF THE FAMILY DEMANDS THAT THE OTHERS CONCEDE TO THEM? _____
   _____
   _____

   EXPLAIN WHY THIS OCCURS: _____
   _____
   _____ (122)

3. "Cessation of drinking is but the _____ step away from a highly strained, abnormal condition. A doctor said to us, 'Years of living with an alcoholic is almost sure to make any _____ or _____ neurotic. The _____ family is, to some extent, ill.' Let families realize, as they start their journey, that all will not be fair weather. _____ in his turn may be footsore and may straggle. There will be alluring shortcuts and by-paths down which they may wander and lose their way."   (122, 123)

4. IF THE FAMILY MEASURES LIFE TODAY AGAINST THAT OF OTHER YEARS AND IT FALLS SHORT, WHAT MAY HAPPEN? _____
   _____ (123)

5. REBUILDING THE FAMILY STRUCTURE MAY TAKE YEARS TO COMPLETE.
   TRUE or FALSE   (123)

6. EXPLAIN HOW WE OBTAIN GROWTH OUT OF PAST ERRORS? _____
   _____
   _____ (124)

7. EXPLAIN HOW THE DARK PAST BECOMES THE GREATEST POSSESSION WE HAVE AS WELL AS THE KEY TO LIFE AND HAPPINESS FOR OTHERS?
   _____
   _____

   THIS IS ALSO A PROMISE.   TRUE or FALSE   (124)

8. UNDER WHAT CONDITIONS DO WE DISCUSS PAST OCCURRENCES?
   _____
   _____ (124, 125)

9. WHEN WE TALK ABOUT OTHERS, HOW SHOULD WE TEMPER THESE DISCUSSIONS? _____
   _____ (125)

10. "Another principle we observe carefully is that we do not relate intimate _____ of another person unless we are sure he would approve. We find it better, when possible, to stick to our _____ stories."   (125)

11. WE ALCOHOLICS ARE SENSITIVE PEOPLE. THE TEXT CONSIDERS THIS A SERIOUS HANDICAP THAT WE NEED TO OUTGROW. TRUE or FALSE (125)

12. "Many alcoholics are enthusiasts. They run to extremes. At the beginning of recovery a man will take, as a _____ , one of _____ directions. He may either plunge into a frantic attempt to get on his _____ in business, or he may be so enthralled by his new life that he _____ or _____ of little else. In either case certain family problems will arise. With these we have had experience galore.
We think it _____ if he rushes headlong at his economic problem." (125, 126)

13. "For us, _____ well-being always followed _____ progress; it _____ preceded.
Since the _____ has suffered more than anything else, it is well that a man exert himself there. He is not likely to get _____ in any direction if he fails to show _____ and _____ under his own roof." (127)

14. WHAT IS THE GUIDING PRINCIPLE FOR A HAPPY FAMILY?
_____
_____
_____
_____ (127, 128)

15. THE NEWLY SOBER ALCOHOLIC MAY TAKE THE PATH OF BECOMING A _____ ENTHUSIAST. (128)

16. "If the family _____ , dad will soon see that he is suffering from a distortion of _____ . He will perceive that his spiritual growth is _____ , that for an average man like himself, a spiritual life which does not _____ his family obligations may not be so perfect after all. If the family will appreciate that dad's current behavior is but a _____ of his development, all will be well. In the midst of an understanding and sympathetic family, these vagaries of dad's spiritual infancy will quickly _____ ." (129)

17. WE BELIEVE GOD WANTS US TO DO WHAT? _____
_____
_____
_____
_____
_____
_____ (130)

18. "One more suggestion: Whether the family has spiritual convictions or not, they may do well to examine the _____ by which the alcoholic member is trying to live. They can hardly fail to _____ these simple principles, though the head of the house still fails somewhat in _____ them. Nothing will help the man who is off on a spiritual tangent so much as the wife who _____ a sane spiritual program, making a better practical use of it." (130)

19. "At the very _____ , the couple ought to frankly _____ the fact that each will have to _____ here and there if the family is going to play an effective part in the new life. Father will necessarily spend much time with other alcoholics, but this activity should be _____ ." (131)

20. SHOULD ALCOHOLICS AVOID RELIGIOUS PEOPLE? _____ (131)

21. "We have been speaking to you of serious, sometimes tragic things. We have been dealing with alcohol in its worst aspect. But we aren't a _____ lot. If _____ could see no _____ or _____ in our existence, they wouldn't want it. We absolutely insist on enjoying life. We try not to indulge in _____ over the state of the nations, nor do we carry the world's troubles on our _____ . When we see a man sinking into the mire that is alcoholism, we give him first _____ and place what we have at his _____ . For his sake, we do recount and almost relive the horrors of our past. But those of us who have tried to shoulder the _____ burden and trouble of others find we are soon _____ by them." (132)

22. WHAT IS THE PROMISE ON PAGE 132? _____
_____
_____
_____ (132)

23. GOD WANTS US TO BE WHAT? A_____
B_____ C_____ (133)

24. DID GOD MAKE PEOPLE BECOME ALCOHOLICS? _____ (133)

25. GOD HAS SUPPLIED US WITH AN ABUNDANT SUPPLY OF FINE DOCTORS, PSYCHOLOGISTS AND PRACTITIONERS OF VARIOUS KINDS? WHEN WE USE THESE PROFESSIONALS AS AN ADJUNCT TO OUR PROGRAM OF RECOVERY, THEY CAN BE A GREAT ASSET.   AGREE or DISAGREE (133)

26. THE ALCOHOLIC WILL WANT TO INVITE THE FAMILY INTO HIS OR HER MORNING MEDITATION. WHETHER THE FAMILY GOES ON A SPIRITUAL SPIRITUAL BASIS OR NOT, THE ALCOHOLIC MEMBER HAS TO IF HE OR SHE WOULD RECOVER.   TRUE or FALSE (134, 135)

27. LIST A.A.'s THREE MOTTOES:
A_____
_____
_____
B_____
_____
_____
C_____
_____
_____ (135)

NOTES

Chapter 10   TO EMPLOYERS

(136 - 150)

1. WHEN THE EMPLOYER FEELS A MORAL RESPONSIBILITY FOR THE WELL-BEING OF EMPLOYEES, A CLEAR UNDERSTANDING OF ALCOHOISM IS A GREAT BENEFIT TOWARD MEETING THAT RESPONSIBILITY.

    TRUE or FALSE   (136, 137)

2. "If you desire to _____ it might be well to _____ your own _____ , or _____ of it. Whether you are a hard drinker, a moderate drinker or a teetotaler, you may have some pretty strong opinions, perhaps prejudices."   (139)

3. "When dealing with an alcoholic there may be a natural _____ that a man could be so _____ , _____ and _____ . Even when you understand the malady better, you may feel this feeling rising."   (139)

4. HAS THE ALCOHOLIC BEEN THE VICTIM OF CROOKED THINKING? _____ CROOKED THINKING IS ANOTHER NAME FOR WHAT? _____ _____ _____ (140)

5. "When drinking, or getting over a bout, an alcoholic, sometimes the model of _____ when normal, will do _____ things. Afterward, his revulsion will be _____ . Nearly always, these antics indicate nothing more than _____ conditions."   (140, 141)

6. IF YOU ARE SURE AN ALCOHOLIC EMPLOYEE DOES NOT WANT TO STOP DRINKING, WHAT SHOULD YOU DO? _____ _____ (141)

7. THERE ARE TEN GENERAL STEPS FOR THE EMPLOYER TO FOLLOW WHEN ASSISTING AN ALCOHOLIC EMPLOYEE TOWARDS RECOVERY. LIST THEM: A _____

    _____

    _____

    _____

    _____

    B _____

    _____

    _____

    _____

    _____

    C _____

    _____

    _____

    _____

    D _____

    _____

    _____

    _____

    _____

E _____

_____

_____

_____

F _____

_____

_____

_____

G _____

_____

_____

_____

H _____

_____

_____

_____

_____

I _____

_____

_____

_____

J _____

_____

_____

_____

_____ (141 – 148)

8. WHAT AMOUNT OF ATTENTION SHOULD AN ALCOHOLIC EMPLOYEE
    RECEIVE AT WORK? _____

    _____

    _____ (149)

9. WILL A RECOVERING ALCOHOLIC WANT SPECIAL ATTENTION? _____ (149)

10. CAN THE EMPLOYER PLAY A BIG PART IN HELPING AN ALCOHOLIC
    RECOVER? _____   (149, 150)

NOTES

NOTES

Chapter 11   A VISION FOR YOU
(151 - 164)

1. WHAT IS ANOTHER INDICATION OF ALCOHOLISM IN A PERSON?
   _____
   _____ (151)

2. ALCOHOLICS BECOME SUBJECTS OF WHOM? _____
   WHAT THEN HAPPENS? _____
   _____ (151)

3. LIST THE FOUR HORSEMEN: A _____
   B_____   C _____
   D_____   (151)

4. IF THE ALCOHOLIC DOES <u>NOT</u> LEARN TO BE HAPPY <u>ABOUT</u> SOBRIETY,
   WHAT WILL OCCUR? _____ (152)

5. GIVE A DEFINITION OF THE MENTAL BOTTOM FOR THE ALCOHOLIC:
   _____
   _____ (152)

6. LIST THE TWELVE PROMISES THAT ARE A SUBSTITUTE FOR LIQUOR:
   A _____
   _____
   B_____
   _____
   C_____
   _____
   D_____
   _____
   E_____
   _____
   F_____
   _____
   G_____
   _____
   H_____
   _____
   I_____
   _____
   J_____
   _____
   K_____
   _____
   L_____
   _____ (152, 153)

7. WHAT IS THE HOPE OF THE AUTHORS OF THE BOOK?
   A_____
   B_____
   _____ (153)

8. GIVE AN EXAMPLE OF THE INSANITY OF THE FIRST DRINK RETURNING:

_____

_____

_____

_____ (154)

9. WILLPOWER CANNOT STOP ALCOHOLISM FOR LONG. WHAT WILL ARREST IT? _____ (155)

10. GOD WILL GIVE ALCOHOLICS MASTERY OVER THEIR PROBLEMS IF THEY DO WHAT? _____ (155, 156)

11. TO MAINTAIN SOBRIETY, THE ALCOHOLIC NEEDS TO KEEP SPIRITUALLY ACTIVE. EXPLAIN HOW? _____

_____

_____ (156)

12. WHAT DOES ALCOHOL DO TO THE BODY AND MIND? _____

_____ (157)

13. WHAT TWO THINGS MUST ALCOHOLICS DO IF THEY WANT TO KEEP THEIR SOBRIETY? A_____

_____

B_____

EXPLAIN HOW THESE TWO THINGS ARE ACCOMPLISHED: _____

_____ (158)

14. "These men had found something brand new in life. Though they knew they _____ help other alcoholics if they would remain _____ , that motive became secondary. It was _____ by the happiness they found in giving themselves for _____ . They shared their homes, their slender resources, and gladly devoted their spare _____ to fellow-sufferers. They were _____ , by day or night, to place a new man in the hospital and _____ him afterward. They grew in numbers. They experienced a few distressing _____ , but in those cases they made an effort to bring the man's _____ into a spiritual way of living, thus relieving much worry and suffering." (159)

15. A.A. MEETINGS ARE PLACES WHERE ALCOHOLICS CAN SHARE THEIR EXPERIENCE, STRENGTH AND HOPE. WHAT ARE TWO OTHER PURPOSES FOR A.A. MEETINGS? A_____

_____

B_____

_____ (159, 160)

16. THE PRIME OBJECT OF A.A. MEETINGS IS TO PROVIDE A TIME AND PLACE WHERE NEW PEOPLE MIGHT BRING THEIR PROBLEMS. IN A REASON-ABLE CONTEXT, CAN WE TALK ABOUT DRUGS AT A.A. MEETINGS?

_____ (160)

17. WHAT IS THE GREAT REALITY? _____

_____

_____

_____ (161)

18. ALCOHOLICS ARE WRECKED IN THE SAME VESSEL. EXPLAIN HOW THEY ARE RESCUED. _____

_____

_____ (161)

19. "Every few days this doctor suggests _____ approach to one of his patients. _____ our work, he can do this with an eye to selecting those who are _____ and able to recover on a _____ _____ . Many of us, former patients, go there to _____." (162)

20. WHAT IS THE PROMISE ON PAGE 163 OF THE TEXT? _____

_____

_____

_____ (163)

21. WHAT ARE THE FIVE PROMISES ON PAGE 164 OF THE TEXT?

A_____

_____

_____

_____

_____

B_____

_____

_____

_____

C_____

_____

_____

_____

D_____

_____

_____

_____

E_____

_____

_____

_____ (164)

22. WHAT IS THE GREAT FACT FOR US? _____

    _____

    _____

    _____

    _____

    _____

    _____

    _____ (164)

23. AS WE LEARNED IN THE FOREWORD TO THE SECOND EDITION, THE BOOK ALCOHOLICS ANONYMOUS IS THE PROGRAM OF RECOVERY. IN CHAPTER TWO THE BOOK SETS FORTH THE THREE BASIC COMPONENTS OF THE PROGRAM: **ATTENDING MEETINGS, PRACTICING THE PRINCIPLES FOUND IN THE TEXT, AND GIVING BACK TO THE FELLOWSHIP THROUGH SERVICE.** IN AN APPARENT CONTRADIC-TION, THE AUTHORS STATE "Our book is meant to be suggestive only." HOWEVER, BY A STUDY OF THE CONTEXT OF THIS STATEMENT, IT IS CLEAR THAT IT IS THE ENTIRE A.A. PROGRAM THAT IS SUGGESTED AS A WAY OF RECOVERY. NO IMPLICATION WAS INTENDED THAT THE A.A. TEXT IS NOT NECESSARY TO RECOVERY.   AGREE or DISAGREE (164)

24. "Abandon yourself to God as you understand God. Admit your faults to Him and to your fellows. Clear away the wreckage of your past. Give freely of what you find and join us. We shall be with you in the Fellowship of the Spirit, and you will surely meet some of us as you trudge the Road of Happy Destiny." ALL TWELVE STEPS ARE IN THIS PASSAGE.   AGREE or DISAGREE (164)

NOTES

NOTES

PERSONAL STORIES   DOCTOR BOB'S NIGHTMARE
(171 - 181)

1. WHAT PLAYED AN IMPORTANT PART IN BRINGING ON BOB'S ALCOHOLISM? _____

    _____

    _____ (172)

2. WHEN DID DRINKING BECOME A MAJOR EXTRA-CURRICULAR ACTIVITY FOR BOB? _____ (172)

3. WHY WAS BOB ELECTED TO MEMBERSHIP IN A DRINKING SOCIETY AT MEDICAL SCHOOL? _____

    _____ (173)

4. WHY DID BOB HAVE TO GO BACK FOR TWO MORE QUARTERS IF HE WANTED TO GRADUATE FROM MEDICAL SCHOOL? _____

    WHAT DID HE HAVE TO DO TO GRADUATE? _____

    _____ (174)

5. HOW DID BOB STAY OUT OF TROUBLE DURING HIS INTERNSHIP?

    _____

    _____

    _____ (174)

6. "When those _____ years were up, I opened an office downtown. I had some money, all the time in the world, and considerable _____ trouble. I soon discovered that a couple of _____ would alleviate my gastric distress, at least for a few hours at a time, so it was not at all difficult for me to return to my former _____ indulgence."   (174)

7.   "After _____ years of this, I wound up in the local _____ where they attempted to help me, but I would get my friends to _____ me a _____ , or I would _____ the _____ about the building, so that I got rapidly worse."   (175)

8. WHY WOULD BOB USE LARGE DOSES OF SEDATIVES IN THE MORNING?

    _____

    _____

    _____

    _____ (176)

9. HOW LONG WAS BOB'S DRINKING CAREER A NIGHTMARE? _____ (177)

10. "I used to promise my wife, my friends, and my children that I would drink no more–promises which seldom kept me sober even through the day, though I was very sincere when I made them."   EXPLAIN WHY BOB COULD NOT KEEP HIS PROMISE: _____

    _____

    _____

    _____ (177)

11. BOB WAS ATTRACTED TO A CROWD OF PEOPLE BECAUSE OF THEIR POISE, HEALTH AND HAPPINESS. WHAT DID THEY HAVE? _____

_____

WHO KEPT BOB INTERESTED IN THESE PEOPLE? _____ (178)

12. " 'What did the man do or say that was different from what others had done or said?' It must be remembered that I had read a great deal and talked to everyone who knew, or thought they knew anything about the subject of _____ . But this was a man who had _____ many years of frightful drinking, who had had most all the drunkard's experiences known to man, but who had been cured by the very means I had been trying to employ, that is to say the _____ approach. He gave me information about the subject of alcoholism which was undoubtedly helpful. *Of far more importance was the fact that he was the first living human with whom I had ever talked, who knew what he was talking about in regard to alcoholism from actual experience. In other words, he talked my language.* He knew all the answers and certainly not because he had picked them up in his reading."
THIS IS WHERE BOB TOOK STEPS ONE AND TWO. TRUE or FALSE (180)

13. "It is a most wonderful blessing to be _____ of the terrible curse with which I was afflicted. My health is good and I have regained my self-respect and the respect of my colleagues. My home life is ideal and my business is as good as can be expected in these uncertain times."
THIS PASSAGE INDICATES THAT BOB CONTINUED TO WORK THE STEPS OF RECOVERY? TRUE or FALSE (180)

14. WHAT ARE THE FOUR REASONS BOB CONTINUED TO WORK STEP TWELVE? A_____
B_____
C_____
_____
D_____
_____ (180, 181)

15. WHAT ARE THREE FORMS OF INTELLECTUAL PRIDE WHICH HINDER A SPIRITUAL APPROACH TO ALCOHOLISM?
A_____
B_____
C_____ (181)

16. WHAT ARE THE TWO PROMISES ON PAGE 181? A_____
_____
_____
_____
_____
_____
_____
_____
B_____
_____ (181)

117

17. <u>APPLICATION</u> OF THE TWELVE STEPS IN OUR LIVES PRODUCES A SPIRITUAL AWAKENING/EXPERIENCE. THE MESSAGE A.A. MEMBERS CARRY IS <u>HOW</u> <u>TO</u> <u>HAVE</u> <u>A</u> <u>SPIRITUAL</u> <u>AWAKENING/EXPERIENCE</u>. THE ORIGINAL FELLOWSHIP PLACED THAT <u>MESSAGE</u> IN WRITTEN FORM IN THE <u>BOOK</u>, ALCOHOLICS ANONYMOUS.   AGREE or DISAGREE

18. THE **MEETINGS** AND THE **PERSONAL** **STORIES** OF OTHER **MEMBERS** HELP US **IDENTIFY**: "Yes, that happened to me;" "Yes, I've felt like that;" "Yes, I believe this program can work for me, too." (xii)   THE STRUCTURE OF THE PROGRAM OF ALCOHOLICS ANONYMOUS, WHICH PROVIDES THE FRAMEWORK BY WHICH TO HAVE A SPIRITUAL AWAKENING/EXPERIENCE, IS FOUND IN THE <u>BOOK</u>, ALCOHOLICS ANONYMOUS; FROM THE TABLE OF CONTENTS THROUGH PAGE 164. TO **FIND** AND **KEEP** **SOBRIETY** WE MUST, LIKE BILL AND BOB, PASS ON WHAT WE HAVE LEARNED TO OTHER ALCOHOLICS. THE PRINCIPLES OF <u>RECOVERY</u> (the 12 Steps of A.A.), THE <u>MEETINGS</u> AND THE CARRYING OF A.A.'s <u>MESSAGE</u>, ARE THE CARE OF GOD. WITH PATIENCE AND PRACTICE, THE CARE OF GOD PRODUCES GOD'S WILL FOR US: "Our real purpose is to fit ourselves to be of maximum service to God and the people about us." (77)   AGREE or DISAGREE

A SPIRITUAL AWAKENING/EXPERIENCE

The spiritual awakening/experience is a deep-down knowledge that we are no longer alone and helpless. It is also an inner assurance that we have learned certain truths which we can now transmit to others so that perhaps they, too, can be helped. We must keep ourselves in constant readiness for the spiritual awakening which always comes to us when we **practice** the **Twelve Steps** of recovery and **surrender** our will to the will of God.

How can I tell if I have had a spiritual awakening/experience? The book, ALCOHOLICS ANONYMOUS, promises that this will occur if we follow and practice its precise instructions. More than that, we can see the evidence in our lives: emotional maturity; an end to constant and corrosive resentments; the ability to love and be loved in return; the belief, even without understanding, that something causes the sun to rise and set, brings forth and ends life, and gives joy to human hearts. With changed lives, we are now able to **do**, **feel**, and **believe** that which we previously could not through our own unaided strength and resources alone. **God** has come into our lives and transformed us **entirely**. This rebirth is the start of the process in which we shed our old ways of living based on self and turn towards our fellow man in a spirit of love, tolerance, understanding and forgiveness. It is the beginning of a journey which lasts a lifetime.

NOTES

THE TWELVE STEPS OF A.A.

1. We admitted we were powerless over alcohol—that our lives had become unmanageable.

2. Came to believe that a Power greater than ourselves could restore us to sanity.

3. Made a decision to turn our will and our lives over to the care of God *as we understood Him.*

4. Made a searching and fearless moral inventory of ourselves.

5. Admitted to God, to ourselves, and to another human being the exact nature of our wrongs.

6. Were entirely ready to have God remove all these defects of character.

7. Humbly asked Him to remove our shortcomings.

8. Made a list of all persons we had harmed, and became willing to make amends to them all.

9. Made direct amends to such people wherever possible, except when to do so would injure them or others.

10. Continued to take personal inventory and when we were wrong promptly admitted it.

11. Sought through prayer and meditation to improve our conscious contact with God *as we understood Him,* praying only for knowledge of His will for us and the power to carry that out.

12. Having had a spiritual awakening as the result of these steps, we tried to carry this message to alcoholics, and to practice these principles in all our affairs.

THE TWELVE TRADITIONS OF A.A.

1. Our common welfare should come first; personal recovery depends upon A.A. unity.

2. For our group purpose there is but one ultimate authority–a loving God as He may express Himself in our group conscience. Our leaders are but trusted servants; they do not govern.

3. The only requirement for A.A. membership is a desire to stop drinking.

4. Each group should be autonomous except in matters affecting other groups or A.A. as a whole.

5. Each group has but one primary purpose–to carry its message to the alcoholic who still suffers.

6. An A.A. group ought never endorse, finance, or lend the A.A. name to any related facility or outside enterprise, lest problems of money, property, and prestige divert us from our primary purpose.

7. Every A.A. group ought to be fully self-supporting, declining outside contributions.

8. Alcoholics Anonymous should remain forever nonprofessional, but our service centers may employ special workers.

9. A.A., as such ought never be organized; but we may create service boards or committees directly responsible to those they serve.

10. Alcoholics Anonymous has no opinion on outside issues; hence the A.A. name ought never be drawn into public controversy.

11. Our public relations policy is based on attraction rather than promotion; we need always maintain personal anonymity at the level of press, radio, and films.

12. Anonymity is the spiritual foundation of all our traditions, ever reminding us to place principles before personalities.

Slips and
Human Nature
by William Duncan Silkworth, MD

January 1947

The mystery of slips is not so deep as it may appear. While it does seem odd that an alcoholic, who has restored himself to a dignified place among his fellowmen and continued dry for years, should suddenly throw all his happiness overboard and find himself again in mortal peril of drowning in liquor, often the reason is simple.

People are inclined to say, "There is something peculiar about alcoholics. They seem to be well, yet at any moment they may turn back to their old ways. You can never be sure."

This is largely twaddle. The alcoholic is a sick person. Under the techniques of Alcoholics Anonymous, he gets well -- that is to say, his disease is arrested. There is nothing unpredictable about him any more than there is anything weird about a person who has arrested diabetes.

Let's get it clear, once and for all, that alcoholics are human beings. Then we can safeguard ourselves intelligently against most slips.

In both professional and lay circles, there is a tendency to label everything that an alcoholic may do as "alcoholic behavior." The truth is, it is simply human nature.

It is very wrong to consider many of the personality traits observed in liquor addicts as peculiar to the alcoholic. Emotional and mental quirks are classified as symptoms of alcoholism merely because alcoholics have them, yet those same quirks can be found among nonalcoholics, too. *Actually, they are symptoms of mankind!*

Of course, the alcoholic himself tends to think of himself as different, somebody special, with unique tendencies and reactions. Many psychiatrists, doctors, and therapists carry the same idea to extremes in their analyses and treatment of alcoholics. Sometimes, they make a complicated mystery of a condition which is found in all human beings, whether they drink whiskey or buttermilk.

To be sure, alcoholism, like every other disease, does manifest itself in some unique ways. It does have a number of baffling peculiarities which differ from those of all other diseases.

At the same time, many of the symptoms and much of the behavior of alcoholism are closely paralleled and even duplicated in other diseases.

The slip is a relapse! It is a relapse that occurs after the alcoholic has stopped drinking and started on the AA program of recovery. Slips usually occur in the early stages of the alcoholic's AA indoctrination, before he has had time to learn enough of the AA technique and AA philosophy to give him a solid footing. But slips may also occur after an alcoholic has been a member of AA for many months or even several years, and it is in this kind, above all, that one finds a marked similarity between the alcoholic's behavior and that of "normal" victims of other diseases.

It happens this way: When a tubercular patient recovers sufficiently to be released from the sanitarium, the doctor gives him careful instructions for the way he is to live when he gets home. He must drink plenty of milk. He must refrain from smoking. He must obey other stringent rules.

For the first several months, perhaps for several years, the patient follows directions. But as his strength increases and he feels fully recovered, he becomes slack. There may come the night when he decides he can stay up until ten o'clock. When he does this, nothing untoward happens. Soon, he is disregarding the directions given him when he left the sanitarium. Eventually, he has a relapse!

The same tragedy can be found in cardiac cases. After the heart attack, the patient is put on a strict rest schedule. Frightened, he naturally follows directions obediently for a long time. He, too, goes to bed early, avoids exercise such as walking upstairs, quits smoking, and leads a Spartan life. Eventually, though, there comes a day, after he has been feeling good for months or several years, when he feels he has regained his strength, and has also recovered from his fright. If the elevator is out of repair one day, he walks up the three flights of stairs. Or he decides to go to a party -- or do just a little smoking -- or take a cocktail or two. If no serious aftereffects follow the first departure from the rigorous schedule prescribed, he may try it again, until he suffers a relapse.

In both cardiac and tubercular cases, the acts which led to the relapses were preceded by wrong thinking. The patient in each case rationalized himself out of a sense of his own perilous reality. He deliberately turned away from his knowledge of the fact that he had been the victim of serious disease. He grew overconfident. He decided he didn't have to follow directions.

Now that is precisely what happens with the alcoholic -- the arrested alcoholic, or the alcoholic in AA who has a slip. Obviously, he decides to take a drink again some time before he actually takes it. He starts thinking wrong before he actually embarks on the course that leads to a slip.

There is no reason to charge the slip to alcoholic behavior or a second heart attack to cardiac behavior. The alcoholic slip is not a symptom of a psychotic condition. There's nothing screwy about it at all. *The patient simply didn't follow directions.*

For the alcoholic, AA offers the directions. A vital factor, or ingredient of the preventive, especially for the alcoholic, is sustained emotion. The alcoholic who learns some of the techniques or the mechanics of AA but misses the philosophy or the spirit may get tired of following directions -- not because he is alcoholic, but because he is human. Rules and regulations irk almost anyone, because they are restraining, prohibitive, negative. The philosophy of AA, however, is positive and provides amply sustained emotion -- a sustained desire to follow directions voluntarily.

In any event, the psychology of the alcoholic is not as different as some people try to make it. The disease has certain physical differences, yes, and the alcoholic has problems peculiar to him, perhaps, in that he has been put on the defensive and consequently has developed frustrations. But in many instances, there is no more reason to be talking about "the alcoholic mind" than there is to try to describe something called "the cardiac mind" or "the TB mind."

I think we'll help the alcoholic more if we can first recognize that he is primarily a human being -- afflicted with human nature.

Why Have a Home Group?

In a recent letter to a member of the Fellowship, a member of the General Service Office staff referred to the home group as the heartbeat of AA. That made a big impression on me, and I believe that just as surely as we are aware of, sensitive to, and in need of our own heartbeat, each of us needs a home group.

It all began in the home group, didn't it? Not all of us readily identified that mysterious group of people who were trying to help us get sober as our home group. In fact, I am painfully aware that the commitment to become a part of anything escapes many in the early stages of recovery.

Most members of the Fellowship will never have the rewarding experience of attending a General Service Conference. Only a few are even touched by our area assemblies, state and national conventions, and other functions which bring members together from many home groups. Even the district functions might be attended by only a small portion of the membership of the groups involved. To many, their AA is only the home group. If this is so, what should the home group be to the member, and why should a member have a home group?

When we took those first faltering steps to recovery, many of us would have stumbled and fallen once again if we had to make what was to be a miraculous change by ourselves. In my case, the first rays of hope came from those sometimes loving, sometimes cantankerous old geezers who sat around the table in my hometown. A long time before I believed, or even heard, what they told me, I began thinking there might be a chance simply because I thought if they could do it, so could I.

The first slogans I heard came from them. Later, when I heard the same things from speakers at a convention, I thought it was so wise; but it was months before I realized that I first heard those thoughts from the fat little guy who I thought was so windy and who eventually became my sponsor. In fact, after I got into service work, I thought I needed to go to conventions, assemblies, and Forums to get my batteries recharged because things were so dull and routine in my home group.

Now I know that it's not the wonderful people I've met from throughout these great lands who have helped keep me sober most of the time, but those wonderful people sitting around the table in my hometown who loved me when I could not love, who waited for me to quit lying, who tolerated me when I would be part of nothing, and who never asked me to leave when I was obnoxious. Because of their love and patience, I was able finally to get outside of myself and make some sort of commitment to the group.

It seems to me that, in the beginning, a home group is all most of us can possibly handle. It's where we first find a sponsor, where someone first sees that we get a Big Book, where we first see the Steps on the wall, where we learn again to pray, and where we first begin to recover. (Remember the heartbeat?) But most of all, because of the trust that develops through the meetings of a home group, it is where we might first begin to care about someone else so that we might eventually begin to love again, both in AA and among our friends and family.

It is where we first learn to take responsibility so that we might eventually take responsibility for our lives. In my case, that began with the simple chore of cleaning out ashtrays. (How wise that they knew I could do no more!) It was there we learned to do Twelfth Step work so that we could eventually pass on to others what was so freely given to us, thereby assuring the very future and survival of the Fellowship. It was there we first learned about the rest of the Fellowship, and someone began answering the questions about all the mysteries of what makes the whole thing work.

Oh yes, the home group is the heartbeat of the Fellowship. There are many reasons why the Fellowship needs these wonderful groups, and there are many reasons why the groups need each and every member running through their life veins. But most important, we need our home groups. That's where it all began, and it's where it will all end for us. Yes, all of us have also had the job of burying some of those people who passed the recovery program on to each of us.

With this week at the Conference, this phase of my service to the Fellowship, of paying back a small measure of my gratitude, begins to wind down. What will I do now? If I am very, very lucky, those who are doing such a marvelous job of serving the Fellowship in my home group might, just might, allow me to make coffee next week and maybe even talk to a drunk.

R.B.
Neosho, Mo.
September 1986

Interdependent

God – Others – Self
A.A. – Steps 10, 11, 12
Carrying the Message of A.A.
or <u>How To Have A Spiritual Awakening</u>.
The <u>Spiritual Malady</u> Is Overcome Which
Relieves <u>The Mental Obsession</u>
One Day At A Time.

Dependent
On A.A.
Text Book, Fellowship, Service, Sponsor, Home Group
Steps – 4, 5, 6, 7, 8, 9
Working on the Mental Obsession

Independent
from Alcohol
Total Abstinence
Join A.A. – Steps 1, 2, 3
Phenomenon of Craving is Arrested
(Physical)

Dependent
on Alcohol
Alcoholism
Physical (Phenomenon of Craving)
and
Mental (Mental Obsession)

The original 100 men and women put the program of Alcoholics Anonymous in written form. They called their Book, ALCOHOLICS ANONYMOUS. The written form or the A.A. Program has three components: The Book, ALCOHOLICS ANONYMOUS - Meetings of Alcoholics Anonymous - Service to Alcoholics Anonymous.

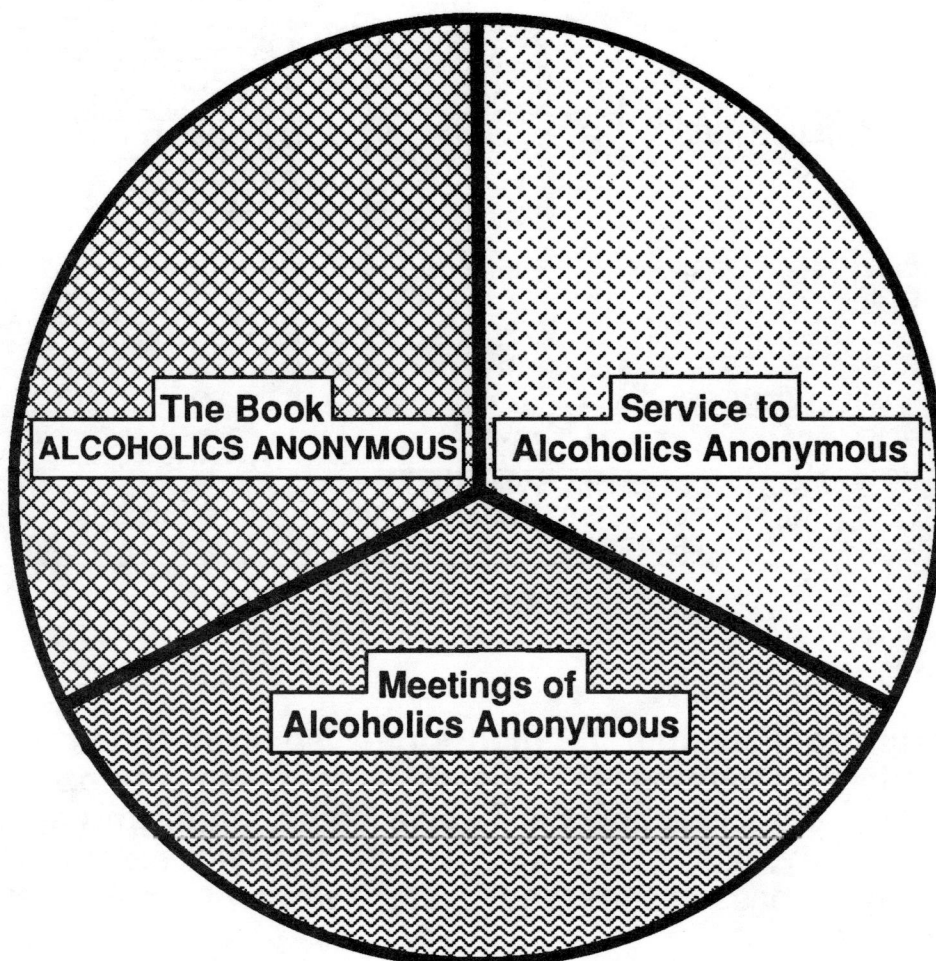

The Book
ALCOHOLICS ANONYMOUS

Service to
Alcoholics Anonymous

Meetings of
Alcoholics Anonymous

RECOVERY

ARCH TO FREEDOM → Pg 47 & 62

(FAITH)

STEPS

(COURAGE) 4 | 3 | 5 (INTEGRITY)

PATH OF SOBRIETY

KEYSTONE
DECISION
Pg 62

(WILLINGNESS) 6 | 7 (HUMILITY)

(LOVE) 8 | 9 (DISCIPLINE)

(HONESTY) | 12 | (HOPE)
FOUNDATION 1 | 2 | **CORNERSTONE**
OF Pg 12 | (SERVICE) | Pg 47 & 56
WILLINGNESS | | **TO BELIEVE**

(PATIENCE) 10 | 11 (AWARENESS)

SOBRIETY !

(" FREEDOM FROM ALCOHOL, THROUGH THE TEACHING
AND PRACTICING OF THE TWELVE STEPS. " BILL W.)

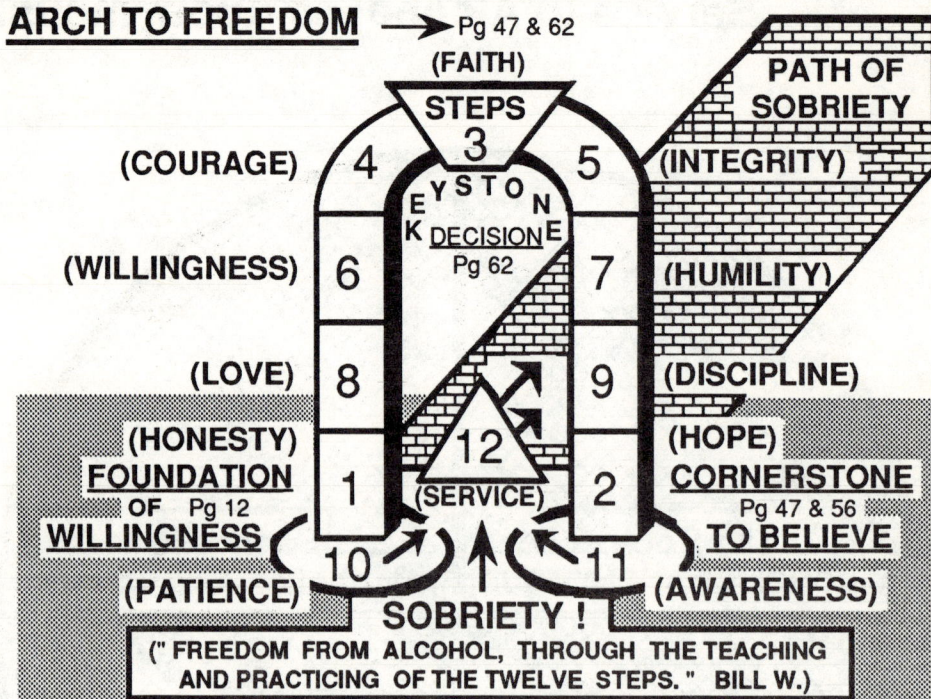

The Arch to Freedom is mentioned several times in the text
"Alcoholics Anonymous." This drawing is an attempt to visually
represent it. Consider how the Twelve Steps, when worked to the best
of one's ability, will form a sturdy arch that will relieve alcoholism.
After we have passed through the arch we can then extend a helping
hand to others.

"Belief in the power of God, plus enough willingness, honesty and humility to establish and maintain the new order of things, were the essential requirements."

ALCOHOLICS ANONYMOUS, pages 13 & 14

START

A **belief** in something; God, A.A. New Idea, etc.
A new person sees A.A. working for others, and might **admit** that A.A. could work for them.
At this point, it's <u>doubtful</u> that they can <u>rely</u> on their belief absolutely.

They need to **act** on their <u>belief</u> or have enough **willingness** to keep coming back to A.A.

If the <u>action</u> is maintained, it begins to remove <u>self-deception</u>, or they grow in their **honesty**.
As the action continues, they begin to understand; they need to attend A.A. regularly.

As their new <u>honesty</u> begins to erode their pride, it produces a degree of **teachability** or **humility**.
This <u>humility</u> pays dividends:
1. A <u>desire</u> to seek the care of A.A.
2. A decision to become <u>active</u> in A.A.

Over time, this process which began with **admission**, will allow them to **accept** or **trust** their original belief.
These are the components for growing in **faith**.
As we <u>act</u> on this process, <u>God</u> grants us the gift of faith.

PAST **PRESENT** **FUTURE**

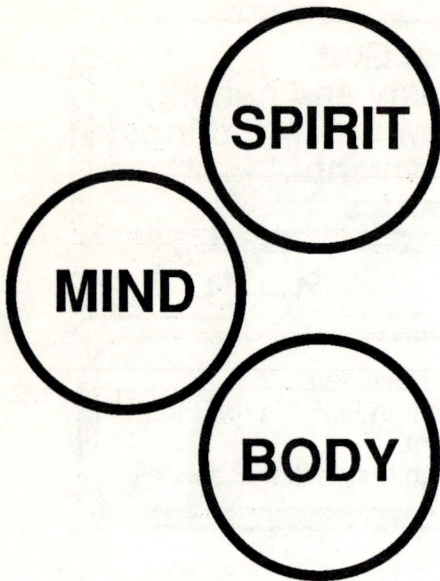

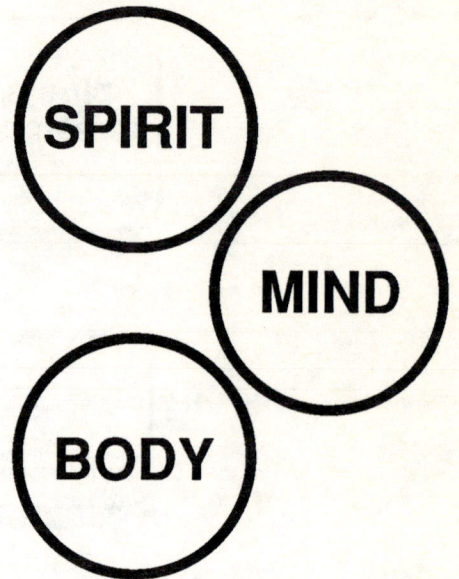

SPIRIT

MIND

BODY

DEPRESSED MIND AND FATIGUED BODY

PAST **PRESENT** **FUTURE**

SPIRIT

MIND

BODY

ANXIOUS MIND AND TENSE BODY

PAST **PRESENT** **FUTURE**

SPIRIT

MIND

BODY

ALERT MIND AND BODY

PAST **PRESENT** **FUTURE**

MEDITATION

1. **ACCEPTABLE ENVIRONMENT**
2. **APPROPRIATE POSTURE**

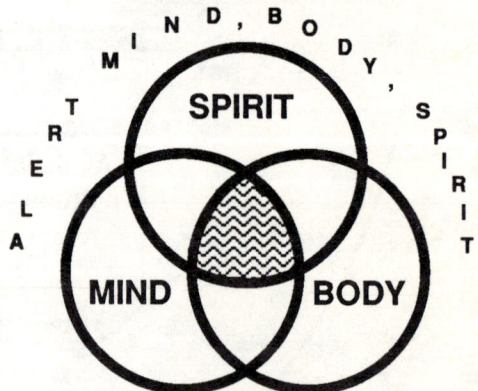

RELATE MIND, BODY, SPIRIT

SPIRIT

MIND BODY

SERENITY

3. **ATTENTIVE BREATHING**
4. **PASSIVE CONCENTRATION**
5. **INVESTMENT IN PRACTICE**

○━━ **INTEGRATION** ━━○

With time and practice, the Twelve Steps of A.A. will cause integration of the body, mind and spirit. See if you can identify how the steps are at work in each of the four sections.

Concept courtesy of
Ralph Spain

New Land

"Arrived at this point, we were squarely confronted with the question of faith. We couldn't duck the issue. Some of us had already walked far over the Bridge of Reason toward the desired shore of faith. The outlines and the promise of the New Land had brought lustre to tired eyes and fresh courage to flagging spirits. Friendly hands had stretched out in welcome. We were grateful that Reason had brought us so far. But somehow, we couldn't quite step ashore. Perhaps we had been leaning too heavily on Reason that last mile and we did not like to lose our support."

Alcoholics Anonymous page 53

"12. Having had a spiritual awakening as the result of these steps, we tried to carry this message to alcoholics and to practice these principles in all our affairs."

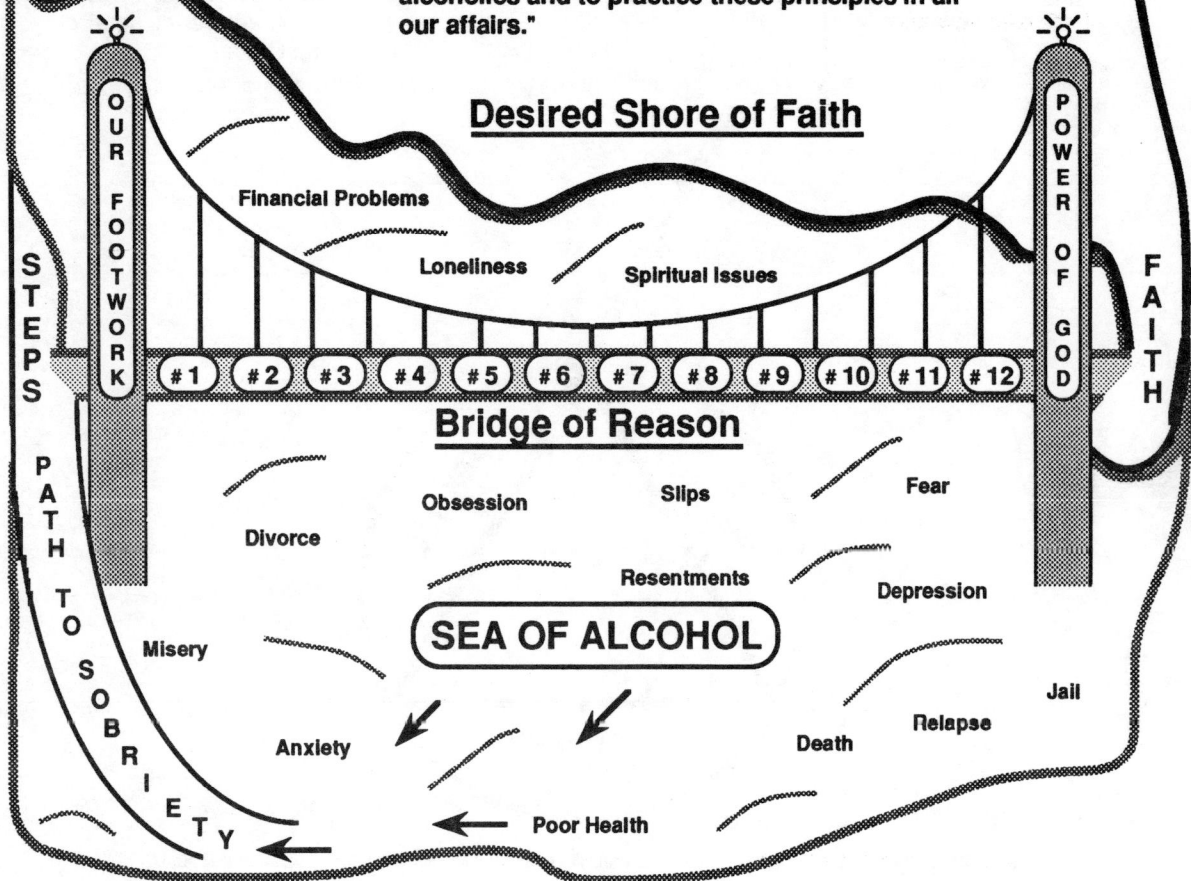

Desired Shore of Faith

OUR FOOTWORK

POWER OF GOD

STEPS PATH TO SOBRIETY

FAITH

Financial Problems

Loneliness

Spiritual Issues

#1 #2 #3 #4 #5 #6 #7 #8 #9 #10 #11 #12

Bridge of Reason

Obsession

Slips

Fear

Divorce

Resentments

Depression

SEA OF ALCOHOL

Misery

Jail

Anxiety

Relapse

Death

Poor Health

THE TRIANGLE GUIDE

For those who question: Am I doing all I can?

Directions: Under each of the headings (recovery, unity, and service), write an honest inventory of your actions. Then put a mark on the line beneath each heading at half inch increments for each item on your list. If you need a longer line, simply extend it. This will help you examine what you are doing for a balanced program.

FOR EXAMPLE:

RECOVERY	UNITY	SERVICE

1. Read the Big Book
2. Work the steps with
    my sponsor
3. Share at meetings
4. Pray to my
    Higher Power
5. Share with newcomers
	1. Support my home group
	2. Observe 7th Tradition
	3. Listen at meetings
	4. Attend many meetings
		1. Cleanup after meetings
		2. Pour coffee
		3. Take people to meetings
		4. Work at Central Office
		5. Work with others
		6. Work on service committees
		7. Work on answering service
		8. Group Officer
		9. Area Assembly

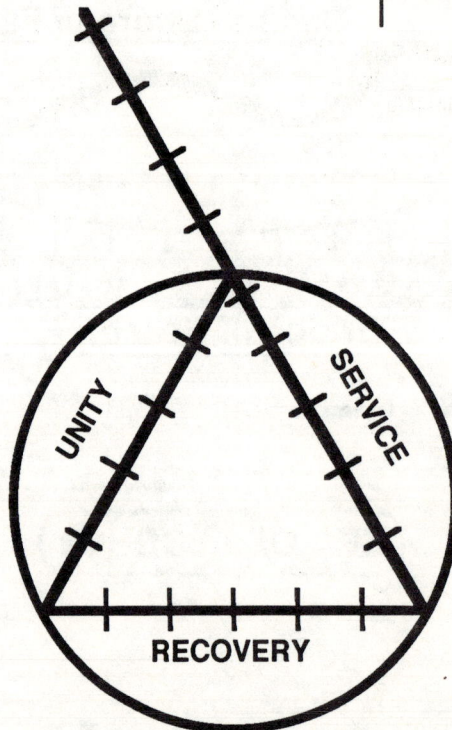

This example might indicate that there could be more emphasis on recovery and unity.

Drawing courtesy of Davi Shewfelt

RESENTMENTS   FEAR   SEX/HARMS

CONDITIONS OR BEHAVIOR

> "Our liquor was but a symptom. So we had to get down to causes and conditions."
> ALCOHOLICS ANONYMOUS, page 64

CONDITIONS OR BEHAVIOR

USEFULNESS: FEELING GOOD AND THE BEHAVIOR ISN'T HARMFUL TO SELF OR OTHERS

CHARACTER DEFECTS: MAY FEEL BAD AND THE BEHAVIOR CAN BE HARMFUL TO SELF AND OTHERS

WE PAUSE WHEN AGITATED OR DOUBTFUL

SEVEN DEADLY SINS
Pride, Greed, Lust, Anger, Gluttony, Envy, Sloth

THINKING OR THE COGNITIVE PROCESSING OF THE BODY'S SENSES

ACTING DIRECTLY ON THE FEAR OR FEELINGS COMING FROM THE INSTINCTS

SELFISHNESS SELF-CENTERED, THE ROOT OF OUR TROUBLES

F E A R
OR THE FEELING OF FEAR

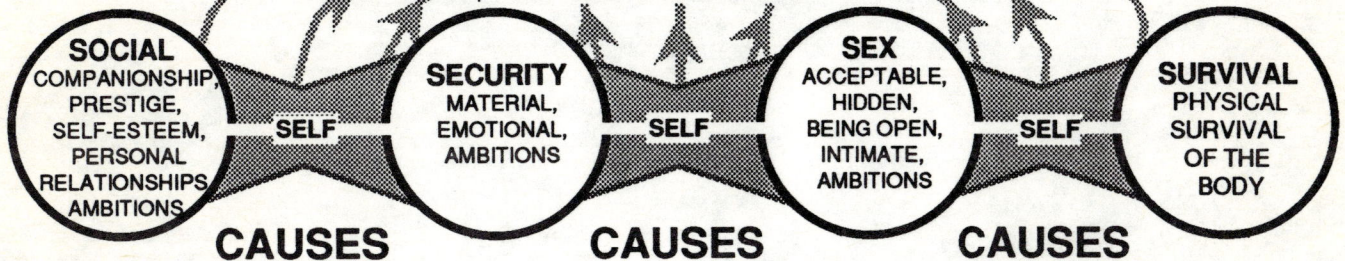

SOCIAL
COMPANIONSHIP, PRESTIGE, SELF-ESTEEM, PERSONAL RELATIONSHIPS, AMBITIONS

SELF

SECURITY
MATERIAL, EMOTIONAL, AMBITIONS

SELF

SEX
ACCEPTABLE, HIDDEN, BEING OPEN, INTIMATE, AMBITIONS

SELF

SURVIVAL
PHYSICAL SURVIVAL OF THE BODY

CAUSES   **CAUSES**   **CAUSES**

SOCIAL INSTINCT	SECURITY INSTINCT	SEX INSTINCT	SURVIVAL INSTINCT
COMPANIONSHIP: Wanting to belong or to be accepted. PRESTIGE: Wanting to be recognized, or to be accepted as a leader. SELF-ESTEEM: What we think of ourselves. PRIDE: An excessive and unjustified opinion of oneself, either positive(self-love) or negative (self-hate). PERSONAL RELATIONSHIPS: Our relations with other human beings and the world around us. AMBITIONS: Our plans to gain acceptance, power, recognition. POWER: Learning, money. BELONGING: Love, friends. FREEDOM: Choices. FUN: Sports, hobbies.	MATERIAL: Wanting money, building, property, clothing, etc. in order to be secure in the future. EMOTIONAL: Based upon our needs for another person or persons. Some tend to dominate, some are overly dependent on others. AMBITION: Our plans to gain material wealth, or to dominate, or to depend upon others. POWER: Learning, money. BELONGING: Love, friends. FREEDOM: Choices. FUN: Sports, hobbies.	PHYSICAL and PSYCHOLOGICAL ACCEPTABLE: Our sex lives as accepted by Society, God's principles or Our own principles. HIDDEN: Our sex lives that are contrary to either Society, God's. principles or Our own principles. AMBITIONS: Our plans regarding our sex lives, either acceptable or hidden. POWER: Learning, money. BELONGING: Love, friends. FREEDOM: Choices. FUN: Sports, hobbies.	PHYSICAL: The body's need for nourishment, exercise and rest. PSYCHOLOGY: The mind's need for mental nourishment, exercise and rest.

INVENTORY FOR RESENTMENTS

1. In dealing with resentments we set them on paper. We listed People, Institutions, or Principles with whom we were angry. (Start with today's memories and work backward from there. Complete Column 1 from top to bottom. Do nothing on Columns 2, 3, 4, or 5 and instruction # 6 until Column 1 is complete.)

2. We asked ourselves why we were angry? (Complete Column 2 from top to bottom. Do nothing on Columns 3, 4, or 5 and instruction # 6 until Column 2 is complete.)

3. On our grudge list we set opposite each name our injuries. Was it our self-esteem, our security, our ambitions, our personal or sex relations which had been interfered with? (Complete each column within Column 3 going from top to bottom. Starting with the Self-Esteem and finishing with the Sexual Ambitions Column. Do nothing on Columns 4, or 5 and instruction # 6 until Column 3 is complete.)

4. Referring to our list again. Putting out of our minds the wrongs others had done, we resolutely looked for our own mistakes. Where had we been selfish, dishonest, self-seeking and frightened and inconsiderate? (Asking ourselves the above questions we complete each column within Column 4. Do nothing on Column 5 or instruction # 6 until Column 4 is complete.)

5. The Inventory was ours, not the others man's. When we saw our faults we listed them. By now we have probably arrived at the following conclusion: that our Character Defects represent Instincts gone astray. Look for the Nature or the Cause, which is one or more of the Instincts causing the condition. (Looking for the affected Instincts, we complete each column within Column 5. Do nothing about instruction # 6 until Column 5 is complete.)

6. Reading from left to right we now see the resentment (Column 1), the cause (Column 2), the part of self that had been affected (Column 3), the symptom of the Nature (Column 4), and the Exact Nature or Cause of Behavior; which are the INSTINCTS (Column 5).

	COLUMN 1 I'm Resentful At:	COLUMN 2 The Cause:	COLUMN 3 WHICH PART OF SELF IS AFFECTED? — Social Instinct — Self-Esteem	Personal Relationships	Ambitions	Security Instinct — Material	Emotional	Ambitions	Sex Instinct — Hidden Sex Relations	Acceptable Sex Relations	Ambitions	COLUMN 4 What is the Symptom of the Nature of our wrongs, faults, mistakes, defect, shortcomings. — Selfish / Prayer	Dishonest	Self-Seeking Frightened	Inconsiderate	COLUMN 5 What is the exact NATURE (Instincts) of our defects, or the CAUSE of behavior — Social	Security	Sexual
1																		
2																		
3																		
4																		
5																		
6																		
7																		
8																		
9																		
10																		
11																		
12																		

NOTES

INVENTORY FOR FEARS

1. In dealing with fears we set them on paper. We listed People, Institutions, or Principles with whom we were fearful. (Start with today's memories and work backward from there. Complete Column 1 from top to bottom. Do nothing on Columns 2, 3, 4, or 5 and instruction # 6 until Column 1 is complete.)

2. We asked ourselves why do we have the fear? (Complete Column 2 from top to bottom. Do nothing on Columns 3, 4, or 5 and instruction # 6 until Column 2 is complete.)

3. Which part of self caused the fear. Was it our self-esteem, our security, our ambitions, our personal or sex relations which had been interfered with? (Complete each column within Column 3 going from top to bottom. Starting with the Self-Esteem and finishing with the Sexual Ambitions Column. Do nothing on Columns 4, or 5 and instruction # 6 until Column 3 is complete.)

4. Referring to our list again. Putting out of our minds the wrongs others had done, we resolutely looked for our own mistakes. Where had we been selfish, dishonest, self-seeking and frightened and inconsiderate? (Asking ourselves the above questions we complete each column within Column 4. Do nothing on Column 5 or instruction # 6 until Column 4 is complete.)

5. The Inventory was ours, not the others man's. When we saw our faults we listed them. By now we have probably arrived at the following conclusion: that our Character Defects represent Instincts gone astray. Look for the Nature or the Cause, which is one or more of the Instincts causing the condition. (Looking for the affected Instincts, we complete each column within Column 5. Do nothing about instruction # 6 until Column 5 is complete.)

6. Reading from left to right we now see the fear (Column 1), why we have the fear (Column 2), the part of self that caused the fear (Column 3), the symptom of the Nature (Column 4), and the Exact Nature or Cause of the Fear and Behavior; which are the INSTINCTS (Column 5).

	COLUMN 1 I'm Fearful Of:	COLUMN 2 Why Do I Have The Fear?	COLUMN 3 WHICH PART OF SELF IS AFFECTED?									COLUMN 4 What is the Symptom of the Nature of our wrongs, faults, mistakes, defect, shortcomings.				COLUMN 5 What is the exact NATURE (Instincts) of our defects, or the CAUSE of behavior
			Social Instinct			Security Instinct			Sex Instinct							
			Self-Esteem	Personal Relationships	Ambitions	Material	Emotional	Ambitions	Hidden Sex Relations	Acceptable Sex Relations	Ambitions	Selfish	Dishonest	Self-Seeking Frightened	Inconsiderate	Social / Security / Sexual
1																Prayer
2																
3																
4																
5																
6																
7																
8																
9																
10																
11																
12																

NOTES

INVENTORY FOR SEX CONDUCT

1. We listed all people we harmed. (Start with today's memories and work backward from there. Complete Column 1 from top to bottom. Do nothing on Columns 2, 3, 4, or 5 and instruction # 6 until Column 1 is complete.)

2. We asked ourselves what we did? (Complete Column 2 from top to bottom. Do nothing on Columns 3, 4, or 5 and instruction # 6 until Column 2 is complete.)

3. Which part of self caused the harm. Was it our self-esteem, our security, our ambitions, our personal or sex relations which caused the harm? (Complete each column within Column 3 going from top to bottom. Starting with the Self-Esteem and finishing with the Sexual Ambitions Column. Do nothing on Columns 4, or 5 and instruction # 6 until Column 3 is complete.)

4. Referring to our list again. Putting out of our minds the wrongs others had done, we resolutely looked for our own mistakes. Where had we been selfish, dishonest, self-seeking and frightened and inconsiderate? (Asking ourselves the above questions we complete each column within Column 4. Do nothing on Column 5 or instruction # 6 until Column 4 is complete.)

5. The Inventory was ours, not the others man's. When we saw our faults we listed them. By now we have probably arrived at the following conclusion: that our Character Defects represent Instincts gone astray. Look for the Nature or the Cause, which is one or more of the Instincts causing the condition. (Looking for the affected Instincts, we complete each column within Column 5. Do nothing about instruction # 6 until Column 5 is complete.)

6. Reading from left to right we now see the harm (Column 1), what we did (Column 2), the part of self that caused the harm (Column 3), the symptom of the Nature (Column 4), and the Exact Nature or Cause of the Harm and Behavior; which are the INSTINCTS (Column 5) that blocked us off from God's will.

#	COLUMN 1 Whom Did I Hurt?	COLUMN 2 What Did I Do?	Self-Esteem	Personal Relationships	Ambitions	Material	Emotional	Ambitions	Hidden Sex Relations	Acceptable Sex Relations	Ambitions	Selfish	Dishonest	Self-Seeking Frightened	Inconsiderate	Social	Security	Sexual
1															P r a y e r			P r a y e r
2																		
3																		P r a y e r
4																		
5																		
6																		
7																		
8																		
9																		
10																		
11																		
12																		

COLUMN 3 — WHICH PART OF SELF IS AFFECTED? (Social Instinct, Security Instinct, Sex Instinct)

COLUMN 4 — What is the Symptom of the Nature of our wrongs, faults, mistakes, defect, shortcomings.

COLUMN 5 — What is the exact NATURE (Instincts) of our defects, or the CAUSE of behavior

NOTES

NOTES

LESSON ANSWERS

PREFACE
1. A text starts with simple information and proceeds to the more complex material.
2. A. That happened to me (actions).
   B. I felt like that (feelings).
   C. I believe this program can work for me (thinking).

FOREWORD TO THE FIRST EDITION
1. The person is drinking.
2. To show other alcoholics precisely how we have recovered.

FOREWORD TO THE SECOND EDITION
1. An alcoholic friend (Ebby T.).
2. Dr. Silkworth.
3. The Oxford Group.
4. How to have a Spiritual Awakening/Experience.

The following passages are from the book Alcoholics Anonymous and will demonstrate the message of A.A.

"It was now time, the struggling groups thought, to place their message and unique experience before the world. This determination bore fruit in the spring of 1939 by the publication of this volume. The membership had then reached about 100 men and women. The fledgling society, which had been nameless, now began to be called Alcoholics Anonymous, from the title of its own book. The flying-blind period ended and A.A. entered a new phase of its pioneering time." (xvii)

We read that the original fellowship placed their <u>message</u> and unique <u>experience</u> before the world. They now called themselves Alcoholics Anonymous; therefore, the original 100 men and women became A.A. and placed their <u>message</u> and <u>experience</u> in book form.

"New groups started up and it was found, to the astonishment of everyone, that A.A.'s message could be transmitted in the mail as well as by word of mouth." (xviii)

After receiving the <u>message</u>, by mail or word of mouth, a sober member can help teach and transmit that message to a new member.

"Our stories disclose in a general way what we used to be like, what happened, and what we are like now. If you have decided you want what we have and are willing to go to any length to get it—then you are ready to take certain steps."(58)

This asks you to decide if you want what A.A. has and if you are willing to go to any lengths to receive that message.

"Reminding ourselves that we have decided to go to any lengths to find a spiritual experience, we ask that we be given strength and direction to do the right thing, no matter what the personal consequences may be."   (79)

The "lengths" of A.A. are the measure of our willingness or <u>finding a spiritual awakening/experience</u> despite personal consequences.

> "12.   Having had a spiritual awakening as the result of these steps, we tried to carry this message to alcoholics, and to practice these principles in all our affairs."   (60)

Application of the Twelve Steps in our lives produces a spiritual awakening/experience. The message A.A. members carry is <u>How To Have A Spiritual Awakening/Experience</u>. The original fellowship placed that <u>message</u> in written form in the <u>book</u> Alcoholics Anonymous.

"Our stories disclose in a general way what we used to be like, what happened, and what we are like now. If you have decided you want what we have and are willing to go to any length to get it-then you are ready to take certain steps." (58)

If you want what A.A. offers, then you must answer two important questions:
A. Do you want a spiritual awakening/experience.
B. Are you willing to work the Steps to receive that awakening/experience.

We could restate the questions this way: if you have decided you want a spiritual awakening/experience and are willing to work the Steps to receive that awakening/experience, then you are ready for Step Three.

5.   A. The large number of recoveries.
      B. Many reunited homes.

FOREWORD TO THE THIRD EDITION
1.   They summarize the A.A. Program.
2.   They trace exactly the same path to recovery that was blazed by the earliest members.
3.   When one alcoholic talks with another alcoholic, sharing experience, strength, and hope.

THE DOCTOR'S OPINION   STEP #1
1.   A. Spiritual.
      B. Altruistic.
      Spiritual - relating to the spirit (taking in from God). Altruistic - concern for others, self-sacrifice. Giving and receiving are vital to a healthy human spirit.
2.   Phenomenon of craving.
3.   A. Calming of the mind; therefore, the feelings improve.
      B. It's the entire A.A. program that calms the mind in sobriety.
4.   Rules.
5.   Mind.
6.   Craving.
7.   Phenomenon of craving.

8. Something the body senses, but the mind cannot understand.
   An analogy would be the human instinct for survival.
   The mind doesn't interpret the bodily instincts directly. The mind tries to understand the body's need for alcohol and becomes restless, irritable and discontented. When the body receives the needed alcohol, the mind calms and the feelings improve.
9. True.
10. Time.
11. A. Change in feelings (feelings).
    B. They realize (thinking).
    C. Reaction to life (actions).
12. Awareness and acceptance of a Power greater than ourselves or "God Consciousness".
13. Contempt prior to investigation.
14. Our weakness is physical (phenomenon of craving) and mental (obsession). We are powerless over both.
15. Admitting complete defeat.
    Defeat means acknowledging in our thoughts and by our actions that we have no power over either the physical or mental aspects of the disease.
16. A. We are struck with an insane urge – a mental obsession.
    B. Joined with the mental obsession is the physical phenomenon of craving – an allergy of the body.
17. We should first help them understand the true nature of alcoholism.
18. A. The true physical and mental nature of the disease.
    B. Whether drinking or abstaining, that person or the alcoholic will not be the same.

Chapter 1   BILL'S STORY   STEP #1

1. Drinking was not yet continuous; drinking assumed more serious proportion; unhappy scenes at home; I was finished; no real employment; liquor was a necessity; this had to stop; I was through; drinking for oblivion; I could eat nothing; returned to the hospital.
2. A. Liquor became a necessity because of the phenomenon of craving (physical). The obsession (mental) caused Bill to think he could handle it.
   B. Despite this, Bill thought he could control his drinking.
3. A. I saw I could not take so much as one drink.
   B. He came home drunk.
4. Such an appalling lack of perspective or lack of proportion of the ability to think straight, concerning the first drink.
5. Yes, sedatives.
6. I was placed in a nationally known hospital.
7. It relieved me somewhat to learn that in alcoholics the will is amazingly weakened. The mental obsession weakened his will. My incredible behavior. The phenomenon of craving forces Bill to drink.
   Inevitably, Bill gets drunk.
8. I returned to the hospital. This was the finish, curtains, it seemed to me.
9. No words can tell of the loneliness and despair I found in that bitter morass of self-pity.   Bill drinks.
10. No.
11. A. A simple religious idea.
    B. A practical program of action.

12. God had done for him what he could not do for himself.
    His will.
13. Believe in a Power greater than myself.
    Bill kept drinking.
14. I was separated from alcohol.
    Bill was withdrawn from alcohol for the last time.
15. Twelve.
16. A. Belief in the Power of God.
    B. Enough willingness.
    C. Honesty.
    D. Humility.
17. We start with a belief; we then decide to take action on that belief. This is willingness. If the action is maintained; self-deception slips away and we develop honesty. The honesty begins to infiltrate our pride to produce a degree of teachability, otherwise known as humility. With time, this process, which began with an admission of helplessness, allows us to rely on our belief. These are the components for growing in faith. For a better understanding of the "Four Essentials," study the chart on page 129 in theWork/Study Guide guide.
18. A. Destruction of self-centeredness.
    B. Electric effect following acceptance.
19. Working with others is imperative.
20. Bill maintained the spiritual experience which lifted him out of hopeless alcoholism by applying the Twelve Steps to every aspect of his life.
21. We perish.
    We will relapse or drink again.

Chapter 2   THERE IS A SOLUTION   STEP #2

1. A. Meetings.
    B. The book (Alcoholics Anonymous).
    C. Action or service.
2. Ten.
3. A. Homes.
    B. Occupations.
    C. Affairs.
4. A. Our constant thought of others.
    B. How we may help meet their needs.
5. To give directions for what we have to do.
6. It may help identify the progressive nature of alcoholism and demonstrate that an alcoholic is no longer a moderate or hard drinker.
7. Our liquor consumption.
    The phenomenon of craving (the physical) causes us to lose control of our liquor consumption.
8. Drugs; high-powered sedatives.
9. Bodily, mental, stop.
10. Mind, body.
11. They want to control the phenomenon of craving (the physical) with their unaided will (the mental obsession). Stated differently, they want to be nonalcoholic.
12. No.
    Over time, willpower cannot control the phenomenon of craving (physical) or the obsession (mental).

13. A. Self-searching.
    B. Leveling of pride.
    C. Confession of shortcomings.
14. A. Going on to the bitter end blotting out the consciousness of our intolerable situation.
    B. Accept spiritual help.
15. A. Dr. Jung.
    B. Vital spiritual experience.
16. A. Ideas (thinking).
    B. Emotions (feelings).
    C. Attitudes (actions and thinking).
17. Willing, honest, try.
18. Religious, bodies.
19. Clear–cut, directions.

Chapter 3   MORE ABOUT ALCOHOLISM   STEP #2

1. They want to control how much they consume <u>and</u> enjoy that amount. In other words, they want to be nonalcoholic.
2. <u>Compulsion</u>: The fact or state of being compelled, or to force.
   <u>Obsession</u>: An idea that overcomes all others or to believe a lie.
   <u>Illusion</u>: To believe something from an outside source which misleads or deceives.
   <u>Delusion</u>: A false belief held as a result of self-deception.
3. We learned that we had to fully concede to our innermost selves that we were alcoholics.
4. A. Self-deception.
   B. Obsession.
5. Try some controlled drinking; then attempt to stop abruptly.
6. Because of the phenomenon of craving.
7. Yes.
8. That their long period of sobriety and self-discipline can qualify them to drink as other people.
9. Peculiar mental twist.
10. Yes.
11. True.
12. The utter inability to leave alcohol alone, no matter how great the necessity or the wish.
13. The mental state that precedes relapse into drinking.
14. He felt irritated that he had to be a salesman for a concern he once owned.
15. That he could control and enjoy his drinking. Suddenly the thought crossed my mind.
16. The experiment went so well he ordered another whiskey and poured it into his milk.
17. Lack of proportion of the ability to think straight concerning the first drink.
    The alcoholic's thinking (will power) will not keep him from the first drink.
    We call this the obsession.
18. Insanely trivial excuse.
19. Alcoholism, both physical and mental.
    The physical (phenomenon of craving) pushes the jay-walker into the street and the mental (obsession) says, "I won't get hurt."
20. No.

21. Fred was happily married, had an attractive personality and was successful.
22. As he crossed the threshold of the dinning room, he thought it would be nice to have a couple of cocktails with dinner. That was all. Nothing more.
23. He had commenced to drink as carelessly as though cocktails were ginger ale.
24. They both drank.
Sobriety based on feelings (good or bad) may be precarious. The stories of Jim and Fred demonstrate that an assessment of sobriety should be based on an alignment of thinking, actions and feelings through the twelve steps of recovery.
25. A. Am I alcoholic?
B. Am I licked this time?
Alcoholics are powerless over alcohol (mental–obsession) and their lives (physical–phenomenon of craving) are unmanageable.
26. Spiritual principles.
27. God - Higher Power.

Chapter 4   WE AGNOSTIC   STEP #2

1. If, when you honestly want to, you find you cannot quit entirely, or if when drinking, you have little control over the amount you take.
The obsession (mental) makes it impossible to quit entirely and the phenomenon of craving (physical) makes controlling the amount impossible.
2. We have no will power over the obsession or the phenomenon of craving.
3. To enable you to find a Power greater than yourself.
4. Yes.
5. A. We commenced to receive results as soon as we laid aside prejudice and were willing to believe in a Power greater than ourselves.
B. We began to be possessed of a new sense of power and direction as soon as we admit the possible existence of a Creative Intelligence, provided we took other simple steps.
6. Do I now believe, or am I even willing to believe, that there is a Power greater than myself?
7. Alcohol.
8. Yes.
9. A. A logical idea (thinking) of what life is about.
B. A degree of stability and usefulness (actions), demonstrated in the way they live.
C. A degree of happiness (feelings).
10. When we wholeheartedly meet a few simple requirements, we will find a new power, peace, happiness, and sense of direction flow into us.
11. Columbus had a belief the world was round. He had the willingness to take action on that belief by asking the Queen for money and ships. By remaining honest to his belief through his actions, Columbus proved the world was not flat. As a result, Columbus received a degree of humility (teachability – the earth really was round). Through this process, Columbus came to rely on his original belief. These are the essential components for growing in faith. For a better understanding of the "Four Essentials," study the chart on page 129 in the Work/Study Guide guide.
12. We must stop doubting the power of God.
13. Examine the evidence of our senses and draw conclusions.
14. Self-imposed, face, God, God.
15. A. Faith.
B. Reason.

16. Where - Deep down within.
    How - Search fearlessly.
17. The fundamental idea of God in every man, woman, and child.
18. A. Sweep away prejudice.
    B. Think honestly.
    C. Search diligently within.
19. When tempted to drink, a great revulsion will rise. Seemingly, we could not drink even if we wanted to. Thus God has restored our sanity.
    If we work the steps of recovery, God provides the ability to think straight automatically and removes our mental obsession to drink.
20. A. Circumstances make us willing to believe.
    B. We humbly offer ourselves to our maker.
    C. With time, we come to know that we have been healed.
21. Yes.
22. A. He (God) comes to all.
    B. We have to honestly search for Him.
23. A state of absolute hopelessness.
24. Fighting, practice, enthusiastically.
25. First.
26. Defiance.
27. Reliance, defiance.
28. Humility, mind.
29. Agree or Disagree.

Chapter 5   HOW IT WORKS   STEP #3

1. Rarely have we seen a person fail who has thoroughly followed our path.
2. To practice rigorous honesty we need to faithfully adhere to the principles in the A.A. program of recovery. Attending meetings, studying the text and taking action on what we learn is the A.A. path to recovery.
3. Without conscious intent to deceive.
4. Spiritual Awakening, Steps, Awakening, Four.
5. The decision of Step Three—to work Step Four.
6. True.
7. A. Step One.
   B. Step Two.
8. A. Being convinced, we were at Step Three.
   B. We are convinced that any life run on self-will can hardly be a success.   OR
      We had to quit playing God.
   C. Next, we decided that hereafter in this drama of life, God was going to be our Director.
   D. We thought well before taking this step making sure we were ready; that we could at last abandon ourselves utterly to Him.
   E. We found it very desirable to take this spiritual step with an understanding person.
   F. The wording was optional, so long as we expressed the idea, voicing it without reservation.
   G. This was only a beginning.
   H. Next we launched out on a course of vigorous action, the first step of which was a personal housecleaning.
9. Delusion, manages.
10. Selfishness/self-centeredness.

11. Our God–given instincts.
12. Work Step Four.
13. A. We have a new Employer.
    B. Being all powerful, He provided what we needed, if we kept close to Him and performed His work well.
    C. Established on such a footing we became less and less interested in ourselves, our little plans and designs.
    D. We became interested in seeing what we could contribute to life.
    E. We felt new power flow in; we enjoyed peace of mind.
    F. We discovered we could face life successfully.
    G. We became conscious of His presence, we began to lose our fear of today, tomorrow or the hereafter.
    H. We were reborn.
    I. This was only a beginning, though if honestly and humbly made, an effect, sometimes a very great one, was felt at once.
14. God, I offer myself to Thee–to build with me and to do with me as Thou wilt. Relieve me of the bondage of self, that I may better do Thy will. Take away my difficulties, that victory over them may bear witness to those I would help of Thy Power, Thy Love, and Thy Way of life. May I do Thy will always!
15. Decision, willingness.
16. Reflection.
17. Care, God, people.
18. Instinct.
19. Think, act.
20. Virtue, admitted, defeat, decision.
21. Dependence upon a Higher Power.
22. Require.
23. A. The misuse of our willpower.
    B. Attempt to bring it into agreement with God's intention for us.
24. We can pause, ask for quiet and, after becoming still, we say; "God grant me the serenity to accept the things I cannot change, courage to change the things I can, and wisdom to know the difference. Thy will, not mine, be done."

Chapter 5   HOW IT WORKS   STEP #4
1. Liquor, cause, conditions.
2. Disclose, unsalable, promptly, regret.
3. Instincts.
4. Instincts, instinct, instincts, instinct, instincts, natural desires, character defects.
5. Sponsor, defects.
6. Instincts.
7. Caused.
8. Spiritual, mentally, physically.
9. Paper.
10. Angry.
11. Angry.
12. Hurt, threatened.
13. Considered.
14. Dominated.
15. Spiritually.
16. List.
17. Listed.

18. Wrongs.
19. Two, dominating, depend.
20. Reducing.
21. Every aspect.
22. Paper.
23. Why.
24. Self-reliance.
25. Rely.
26. Courage.
27. Attention.
28. Outgrow.
29. Our spiritual awakening allows us to trust and rely on God. Our real purpose is to fit ourselves to be of maximum service to God and the people about us.
30. A. Pride. B. Greed. C. Lust. D. Anger. E. Gluttony. F. Envy. G. Sloth.
31. Pride.
32. Seven deadly sins.
33. A. They trust their God.
     B. They never apologize for God.
     C. They let Him demonstrate, through them, what He can do.
     D. They ask Him to remove their fear and direct their attention to what He would have them be.
34. A. A brand-new kind of confidence is born.
     B. A sense of relief at finally facing ourselves.
     To receive these fruits, we must PERSIST.
35. Sensible.
36. Conduct.
37. Fault.
38. Sane.
39. Selfish, not.
40. Ideals.
41. God.
42. God.
43. Motives, conduct, harm, drink, theorizing.
44. Sanity.
45. Analyzed.
46. Grosser.
47. Thoroughness.
48. Our written inventory, or our Fourth Step.

Chapter 6   INTO TO ACTION   STEP #5
1. Thinking, action, talk.
2. Defects, God.
3. We will get rid of that terrible sense of isolation we have always had.
4. A true kinship with man and God.
5. By doing Step Five.
6. A. Humility is a clear recognition of what and who we really are, followed by a sincere attempt to become what we could be.
    B. Recognizing our deficiencies.
7. Advice, direction, thinking.

8. A. Somehow, being alone with God doesn't seem as embarrassing as facing up to another person. Until we actually sit down and talk aloud about what we have so long hidden, our willingness to clean house is still largely theoretical.
    B. What comes to us alone may be garbled by our own rationalization and wishful thinking.
9. Willpower.
10. An open and honest sharing of our terrible burden of guilt, or Step Five.
11. Exact nature, defects.
12. Vital, facts.
13. Drunk.
14. Closed-mouthed, understanding.
15. A. We are delighted.
    B. We can look the world in the eye.
    C. We can be alone at perfect peace and ease.
    D. Our fears fall from us.
    E. We begin to feel the nearness of our Creator.
    F. We may have had certain spiritual beliefs, but now we begin to have a spiritual experience.
    G. The feeling that the drink problem has disappeared will often come strongly.
    H. We feel we are on the Broad Highway.
    I. We feel we are walking hand in hand with the Spirit of the Universe.
16. After we take Step Five.
17. A. We find a place where we can be quiet for an hour, carefully reviewing what we have done.
    B. We thank God from the bottom of our heart that we know Him better.
    C. Taking this book down from our shelf we turn to the page which contains the twelve steps. Carefully reading the first five proposals we ask if we have omitted anything, for we are building an arch through which we shall walk a free man at last.
    D. We ask whether our work so far is solid.
    E. We ask whether the stones are properly in place.
    F. We ask whether we have skimped on the cement put into the foundation.
    G. We ask whether we have tried to make mortar out of sand. If we can answer to our satisfaction, we then look at Step Six.
18. Look at Step Six.

Chapter 6   INTO ACTION   Step #6
1. Willingness.
2. Learning to do something gladly.
3. Admitted, objectionable.
4. We ask God to help us be willing to allow Him to remove our defects.
5. We have willingly and honestly worked Step Six on all our faults, without any reservations whatever.
    A man or woman who is sincerely trying to grow in the image and likeness of his or her own Creator.
6. A. We must be willing to clean house.
    B. We need to ask God to remove the obsession.
7. Humbled, alcohol, expel.
8. Design, alcohol, instincts.
9. Desires, blindly, willfully, character defects.

10. An attitude of continual readiness to have our defects removed.
11. No, I can't give this up yet.
12. Instincts, grace, of, God.
13. A. Pride. B. Greed. C. Lust. D. Anger. E. Gluttony. F. Envy. G. Sloth.
14. Some of our defects.
15. A one syllable word for procrastination (physically, mentally and spiritually lazy).
16. Perfection, by, self, perfect.
17. A. The Twelve Steps of A.A.
    B. Our progress.
18. Perfection, direction.
19. Our minds close against the grace of God.
    This may be fatal because it is the grace and power of God which arrest and relieve our obsession to drink. No human power can relieve alcoholism. For the alcoholic, to drink is to perish.
20. Agree or Disagree.

Chapter 6   INTO TO ACTION   Step #7
1. My Creator, I am now willing that you should have all of me, good and bad. I pray that you now remove from me every single defect of character which stands in the way of my usefulness to you and my fellows. Grant me strength, as I go out from here, to do your bidding. Amen.
2. Action.
3. Humility.
4. Character - building or developing honesty, tolerance, and true love of man and God.
5. A desire to seek and do God's will.
6. Character flaws, must.
7. Serenity.
8. Life, humility.
9. A change in our attitude toward God can occur.
10. Bludgeoned, beaten, voluntary, turning point.
11. Character defects, unreasonable demands.
12. Self-centered fear.
    A fear that we would lose something we already possessed or would fail to get something we demanded.
13. Demands, disturbance, frustration, reducing.
14. Attitude, humility, humility.
15. Agree or Disagree.
16. Agree or Disagree.

Chapter 6   INTO ACTION   Step #8
1. When we took our inventory.
2. Repair, damage, past.
3. Debris, self-will, show ourselves.
4. Will, beginning, victory, alcohol.
5. A. We look backward to discover where we have been at fault.
   B. We make a vigorous attempt to repair the damage.
   C. Having cleaned away the debris of the past, we consider how, with our knowledge of ourselves, we may develop the best possible relations with every human being we know.

6. Pain, lessened, forgiveness, defensive, wrongs, resentfully, focus, his, excuse, minimizing, forgetting.
7. Unaware, fear, pride, all.
8. Purposeful forgetting is clinging to the idea that while drinking we never hurt anybody but ourselves. Fear tells us: "we dare not proceed" and pride says: "we have no need to." So with conscious awareness, we push our responsibility for some of our past actions out of our minds; believing that amends are not necessary.
   To change our attitude we must make a deep and honest search of our motives and actions.
9. Great, emotional, forgotten, consciousness, emotions, personalities, lives.
10. Defective relations with other human beings.
    Since our purpose is to serve God and the people about us, defective relationships with people represent our distance from God. Our alcoholism develops from running our lives on self-will. It is the grace of God which removes self-centeredness and provides the defense against the first drink. To find the grace of God, we submit to His care and direction through the structure of Alcoholics Anonymous.
11. Instincts, physical, mental, emotional, spiritual, tempers, lie, cheat, sex.
12. Human, personality, memory.
13. A. Admitting the things we have done.
    B. Forgiving the wrongs done us, real or fancied.
    C. Avoiding extreme judgments of ourselves and others.
    D. Avoiding the exaggeration of our defects or others.
    E. Aiming steadfastly for a quiet objective view.
14. It will be the beginning of the end of isolation from our fellows and from God.

Chapter 6   INTO ACTION   STEP #9
1. To fit ourselves to be of maximum service to God and the people about us.
   We fill our purpose by working the Steps to receive a spiritual awakening. To maintain our purpose, we then carry the A.A. message to other alcoholics and practice these principles in all our affairs.
2. Sincere, demonstration, talk.
3. Tact, common sense.
4. Criticize, past, not, our.
5. We may drink if we are afraid to face them.
6. A. We decided to go to any lengths to find a spiritual experience.
   B. We ask that we be given strength and direction to do the right thing, no matter what the personal consequences may be.
7. Consent, others, God.
8. Domestic, alcoholics, fundamentally.
9. A. We are sorry for what we have done.
   B. God willing, we will not repeat the conduct.
10. Sober, good.
11. Unthinking.
12. We have to live it.
    This is accomplished through the Twelve Steps of recovery. We first work the Twelve Steps to receive a spiritual awakening. Then we maintain this awakening by carrying the A.A. message to other alcoholics and practicing A.A. principles in all our affairs.

13.   A. Be sensible.
       B. Be tactful.
       C. Be considerate.
       D. Be humble.
       God's.
14.   Painstaking, amazed.
15.   Twelve.
16.   Work, them.
17.   A. Good judgment.
       B. A careful sense of timing.
       C. Courage.
       D. Prudence.
18.   A. Amends we make now.
       B. Amends we will make later.
       C. Amends we might make or are uncertain of making.
       D. Amends we intend never to make.
19.   Willing, own, mind, others.
20.   Finished, laurels, skip.
       Laurels: honor and glory won for past achievement.
21.   Yes.
       The only exceptions we will make will be cases where our disclosure would
       cause actual harm to others.
22.   One, complete, full.
23.   A. Sponsor.
       B. Spiritual adviser.
       C. God.
       We must do the right thing when it becomes clear, cost what it may.
24.   Complete, willingness, fast, far.
25.   Afraid.
26.   A. The readiness to take the full consequences for past acts.
       B. At the same time, the readiness to take responsibility for the well-being
          of others.

Chapter 6   INTO ACTION   Step #10
   1. Personal, right, past.
       Agree or Disagree.
       Agree or Disagree.
   2. The world of the Spirit.
       To grow in understanding and effectiveness.
       We achieved a degree of understanding and effectiveness as we progressed
       through the first nine steps. Step Ten is the maintenance of the first nine steps
       and the willingness to do Step Eleven. We grow in understanding and
       effectiveness as we work through Steps Ten and Eleven.
   3. Lifetime, resentment.
       Agree or Disagree.
   4. God.
       Agree or Disagree.
   5. Discuss, amends.
   6. Thoughts.
       Agree or Disagree.
       Agree or Disagree.

7. Twenty six.
8. Action, laurels.
9. By growing in understanding and effectiveness.
10. We must carry a vision of God's will into all of our activities and ask how we can best serve God. His will must be done, not ours. These are the thoughts that must go with us.
   The will is the thought-life of an individual.
11. Focusing our will (thinking) on what God would have us think and do.
12. God-consciousness.
   A. Strength.
   B. Inspiration.
   C. Direction.
13. If we have carefully followed directions.
14. We must go further; that means more action.
15. Living, sober, emotional, all.
   Agree or Disagree.
16. Self-searching, admit, accept, correct.
17. An emotional hangover is the direct result of the excesses of the negative emotions (e.g., anger, fear, jealousy) of yesterday and today.
   These errors, if they are to be taken care of, must be admitted and corrected immediately.
18. A. Spot-check inventory – taken at any time of the day, whenever we find ourselves getting tangled up.
   B. End of the day inventory – taken before retiring, where we constructively review our day.
   C. Annual or semiannual inventory – where we make a careful review of our progress since the last such inventory.
19. Axiom: a self-evident truth. When we are disturbed, no matter what the cause, there is something wrong with us. We must look within ourselves for the reason and answer.
20. Quick, balance, self-restraint, analysis, willingness, admit, ours, forgive.
21. Developing self-restraint.
   By avoiding quick-tempered criticism and furious, power-driven arguments.
   We need to train ourselves to physically pause and think and become emotionally calm, then ask God to direct our thinking and actions. We need to do this until the habit of self-restraint becomes automatic.
22. We need to exercise special vigilance by remembering that we are sober only by the grace of God and that any success we may be having is far more His success than ours.
23. Emotionally, wrong, tolerance, love, angry, growing up.
24. We begin to practice justice and courtesy, perhaps going out of our way to understand and help them. We ask ourselves, "Are we doing to others as we would have them do to us--today?"
25. Something right.
26. A. The pains of drinking.
   B. Emotional turmoil.
27. Rationalization.
   Rationalization justifies conduct which is really wrong. The temptation here is to imagine that we had good motives and reasons when we really didn't.
   Rationalization is giving a socially acceptable reason for socially unacceptable behavior, and socially unacceptable behavior is a form of insanity.

28. We think they need to be "taught a lesson," when we really want to punish.
29. Sympathy, attention, mind, emotion, motive, good, act, thought.
30. Learning daily to spot, admit, and correct our character flaws. An honest regret for harms done, genuine gratitude for blessings received, and a willingness to try for better things tomorrow will be the permanent assets we shall seek.
31. Omitting, well done, God, conscience.

Chapter 6   INTO ACTION   Step #11
1. Attitude, work.
2. Constructively review our day.
3. True.
4. After our review we ask God's forgiveness and inquire what corrective measures should be taken.
   A day properly ended gives us a quiet rest which allows us to start the next day in a calm mental state.
5. A. Thinking.
   B. Actions.
6. Brains, use.
7. When our thinking is cleared of wrong motives.
8. A. We ask God for inspiration, an intuitive thought or a decision.
   B. We relax and take it easy.
   C. We don't struggle.
9. A. We pray that we be shown all through the day what our next step is to be.
   B. We pray that we be given whatever we need to take care of our problems.
   C. We ask especially for freedom from self-will.
   D. We are careful to make no request for ourselves only.
   E. We may ask for ourselves, however, if others will be helped.
   F. We are careful never to pray for our own selfish ends.
10. Yes, if circumstances warrant.
11. Books, quick, religious.
12. A. We pause (physically and mentally).
    B. When calm (physically and mentally), we ask for the right thought or action.
13. Agree or Disagree.
14. Prayer and meditation.
15. A. Certain newcomers.
    B. One-time agnostics.
16. Refused, wrong, experiment, tried.
17. Minds, emotions, intuitions, soul.
18. A. Self-examination.
    B. Meditation.
    C. Prayer.
19. The ultimate reality which is God's kingdom.
20. Destiny, try, find, do.
21. Darkness, sunlight.
22. Consider the Eleventh Step Prayer.
23. No.

24. Imagination, constructive, envisions, objectives.
    We have had inner experience with this already. When we are resentful we involve all five of the bodily senses. In meditation or constructive imagination we need to do the same. As we envision our spiritual objective we move deeper into meditation by becoming aware of the bodily senses. This type of meditation can fill the spirit and supply a tremendous enthusiasm for life.
25. Emotional balance.
26. Petition, God.
27. Understanding, carry.
    We are asking God to guide our thoughts and actions.
28. Pause so we can find calm.
    By repeating to ourselves a particular prayer or phrase till the anger, fear, frustration, or misunderstanding has passed. Now we can look for God's will, not ours.
29. A. The belief that God gives explicit guidance on all matters. Frequently, we are listening to our own will in the form of wishful thinking.
    B. The idea that we know God's will for others. This implies a certain amount of presumption and conceit in us.
30. Question, knowledge, experience, persisted, strength, wisdom, mind.
31. That "...God does move in a mysterious way His wonders to perform."
    Our conviction grows as we improve our conscious contact with God. Our affairs may take a remarkable and unexpected turn for the better. Out of grief and suffering, new lessons for living and new resources of courage are uncovered. As we learn to trust God, our conviction becomes real; God is working in our lives.
32. The sense of belonging that comes to us.
33. God watches over us.
    We need to turn to Him and then all will be well with us, here and hereafter.
34. Agree or Disagree.

Chapter 7   WORKING WITH OTHERS   Step #12
1. Intensive work with other alcoholics.
2. Cooperate, criticize, aim.
3. Prospect, him, drinking, time, persuade.
   You may spoil a later opportunity.
4. Have a good talk with the person most interested in them. Get an idea of their behavior, their problems, their background, the seriousness of their condition, and their religious leanings. You need this information to put yourself in their place, to see how you would like someone to approach you if the tables were turned.
5. No.
6. General conversation.
7. Alcoholic, sick, mental twist, drink.
8. Alcoholic, feature, malady, mental, book, alcoholic, conclusion.
   Agree or Disagree.
9. Fatal, body, mind.
10. Protege, admitted, well.
11. Spiritual, agnostic, atheist, sense, Power, spiritual.

12. Must, self-sacrifice, action.
   We have worked the first eleven steps and received our spiritual awakening. We now maintain this spiritual awakening in Steps Ten, Eleven and Twelve. As we have been freely given the message of A.A., we now pass it to someone else. Learning to receive and give is what makes faith real and life worthwhile.

13. General principles common to most denominations.

14. Action, past.
   By working all twelve steps. We learn to trust God, clean house and help others. Growing in understanding of the steps makes helping others a joy. We begin to truly realize how important it is to work with others. This truth helps us comprehend another spiritual truth – we need each other to perform God's will.

15. You have.

16. Book.

17. A. Our Text Book.
   B. Our Fellowship.
   C. Service.

18. Sincerely, read this book, must decide, pushed, prodded, God.

19. No.
   If we leave such persons alone, they may soon become convinced that they cannot recover by themselves. To spend too much time on any one situation is to deny some other alcoholic an opportunity to live and be happy.

20. Yes.
   Out of our experience on the road to recovery we can help others where a nonalcoholic could not.

21. Responsibilities, sure, foundation, enough, every day.
   It may mean loss of sleep, interference with your pleasures, interruptions at work. It may mean sharing your money and home, counseling frantic people, and many other occasions that will inconvenience you.

22. Seldom.

23. People, God.
   True.

24. The idea that he can get well regardless of anyone.
   He must trust in God and clean house.

25. A. The alcoholic should be sure of his recovery.
   B. The time to reunite will be apparent to both.

26. You, new, spiritual progress, persist, back, God's, hands, dictates, circumstances.

27. We can do all sorts of things alcoholics are not supposed to do.

28. They still have an alcoholic mind; there is something the matter with their spiritual status.

29. We must have a legitimate reason for being there.

30. A. Do we have any good social, business, or personal reason for going to this affair?
   B. Do we expect to steal a little vicarious pleasure from the atmosphere of such affairs?

31. Are we trying to regain the experiences or recapture the feelings from past drinking affairs?

32. To be at the place where we may be of maximum helpfulness to others.
   We must never hesitate to go anywhere if we can be helpful.

33. Drinking.

34. Problems, symbol, fighting. We have to!

35. A. Newcomer. B. Prospect. C. Protege. D. Friend. E. New Man.
    F. Green Recruit.
36. Agree or Disagree.
37. Action.
38. By practicing all Twelve Steps of our program.
39. As a result of practicing all Twelve Steps of A.A.
40. A. A person has become able to do, feel, and believe that which he could not
       do before on his unaided strength and resources alone.
    B. A person has been granted a gift which amounts to a new state of
       consciousness and being.
    C. A person has been set on a path which tells him he is really going
       somewhere, that life is not a dead end, not something to be endured or
       mastered.
    D. A person has been transformed, because he has laid hold of a source of
       strength which, in one way or another, he had hitherto denied himself.
    E. A person finds himself in possession of a degree of honesty, tolerance,
       unselfishness, peace of mind, and love of which he had thought himself
       quite incapable.
41. Agree or Disagree.
42. List some thoughts.
43. Doubter, spiritual angle, group, God, name.
44. We must carry the A.A. message to another alcoholic. In this manner the
    spiritual energy is released, which allows us to practice A.A. principles in all
    our affairs. This energy and action is the magnificent reality of Alcoholics
    Anonymous.
45. A. Taking a deep satisfaction and joy in a Twelfth Step job well done.
    B. The opportunity to watch the eyes of men and women open with wonder as
       they move from darkness into light.
    C. Watching lives quickly fill with new purpose and meaning.
    D. Watching whole families reassembled.
    E. Watching alcoholic outcasts received back into their community in full
       citizenship.
    F. Watching these people awaken to the presence of a loving God in their lives.
46. Sobered, relapse, discouraged, elated, temptation, possessive, advice,
    competent, rejected, accepted, they, trust, temptation, rebuffs, take,
    clearly realize, up, good, entire, answers.
47. Whole, alcoholics.
48. Short, taking, indifference, congratulate, grow, feel satisfied, few, two,
    two-stepping.
49. Staying sober on Step One and the first part of the Twelfth Step.
    As it wears off and things go disappointingly dull, some may think A.A. doesn't
    pay off after all.
50. Now, God, calamities, assets, switch, willing, catastrophe.
51. No.
    An honest effort to practice these principles in all our affairs. Well-grounded
    A.A.'s seem to have the ability, by God's grace, to take these troubles in stride
    and turn them into demonstrations of faith.
52. More spiritual development.
53. Our attitudes toward our instincts need to undergo a drastic revision. We learn
    that the satisfaction of instincts cannot be the sole end and aim of our lives. If
    we place instincts first, we shall be pulled backward into disillusionment.

54. We need to place spiritual growth first–then and only then do we have a real chance.

55. As we develop in A.A., we discover that the best possible source of emotional stability is God Himself.

56. Unusual, happily, emotional.

57. Single, good, spiritual, difficulties, solid, spiritual, mental, emotional, fact, sure, possible.

58. Yes.
    A symbol of pleasure and self-importance.
    They were sharply reversed, often they go much too far in the opposite direction. We will need a balanced outlook concerning financial matters.

59. With the help of A.A.'s Twelve Steps, we develop a dependence upon God which will solve our problem.

60. No.
    Our Spiritual condition.

61. Traits, childish, emotionally, grandiose.

62. Yes.

63. Fear.
    To cover up our deep-lying inferiorities.

64. Well-matured, restored, dominate, rule, self-importance, praised, love, service.

65. A deep desire to live usefully and walk humbly under the grace of God.
    Having had a spiritual awakening, as the result of these steps, we tried to carry this message to alcoholics, and to practice these principles in all our affairs, or to fit ourselves to be of maximum service to God and the people about us.

66. By accepting and solving our problems through spiritual principles.

67. With new understanding, we can begin to practice our new principles and in time our attitudes will be transformed.

68. Agree or Disagree.

Chapter 8   TO WIVES

1. Yes.

2. This chapter will help the spouse analyze his or her mistakes while coping with the alcoholic and it will demonstrate that there is hope for the alcoholic.

3. The nature of the alcoholic illness.

4. An alcoholic who has thoroughly bad intentions.
   You can leave that person.
   Such a person has no right to ruin the lives of others, especially children, when there is a way out if the price is paid.

5. CATEGORY ONE: These alcoholics are heavy drinkers. They may drink constantly; they may drink heavily on occasion; they spend too much money on liquor; they may be deteriorating mentally and physically; they may be a source of embarrassment; they are positive they can handle their liquor; they believe liquor will not harm them; they would be insulted if called alcoholic.

6. CATEGORY TWO: These alcoholics show a lack of control over their liquor; they get entirely out-of-hand when drinking; they may admit they have a problem and are positive they will do better; they try to moderate or stay dry; they lose friends; they worry about not drinking like others; they drink in the morning for their nerves; they are remorseful and announce that they want to stop; when feeling better they believe they can moderate their drinking.

7. True.

8. <u>CATEGORY THREE</u>: These alcoholics have become worse than category 2; they have lost more friends; their homes and jobs are wrecks; doctors may have been called in; they may go to sanitariums and hospitals; they admit they cannot drink like others but wonder why; they cling to the notion that they will find a way to control their liquor; they may want to stop but cannot.

9. <u>CATEGORY FOUR</u>: These alcoholics may have been placed in an institution; they may be violent; they appear definitely insane when drunk; they may drink on the way home from the hospital; their doctors have given up and advise that they be committed to an institution; they may have already been committed.

10. Category three.
    Category one.

11. A. The first principle of success is not to get angry at them.
    B. Do not tell them what they must do about their drinking.
    C. Be determined that their drinking is not going to spoil your relations with your children or friends.
    D. Do not set your heart on reforming them.

12. For a friendly talk about their alcohol problem.

13. Suggest, book, confidence, interesting.

14. Drop the subject and try helping the spouse of another alcoholic.

15. Two, apply, binge, not, ask, book, alcoholism, stories, read, spiritual, remedy.

16. Leave them alone.

17. Luck, certain, volume, book, long, crowd, book, normal.

18. Fourth, exceptions, disorders, book, mental, committed, released, power, reverse, dangerous, doctor.

19. Barriers which have sprung between you and your friends will disappear with the growth of sympathetic understanding. You will no longer be self-conscious or feel that you must apologize as though your spouse were a weak character.

20. No.
    Let the alcoholic explain to his or her employer.

21. God can solve your problems, including alcoholism.

22. Everybody, pride, self-pity, vanity, self-centered, selfishness, dishonesty, spiritual.

23. Yes.

24. That we do not disagree in a resentful or critical spirit.

25. The privilege to disengage: "This discussion is getting serious. I'm sorry I got disturbed. Let's talk about it later."

26. Sobriety, Patience, tolerance, understanding, love, rule, own.

27. Resentment, cure, book, alcoholic, power.

28. We try to pause and count our blessings. We become grateful.

29. Jealous, yours, sobriety.

30. We can assist our spouse as he or she works with a new alcoholic friend.
    We can direct our thoughts to the spouse of that new friend, for they also need counsel and love.

31. A. Their lives will be fuller.
    B. They will lose the old life to find one much better.

32. They must redouble their spiritual activities if they expect to survive.
    A spiritual deficiency.

33. An insanely trivial excuse to drink.

34. No.
    They will notice your attempts to shield them. If they get drunk, you are not to blame and you do not have to carry any guilt.

35. God.
36. In God's hands.
37. Direction, advice, experience, painful, hard, understand, difficulties.

Chapter 9   THE FAMILY AFTERWARD
1. A common ground of tolerance, understanding and love.
2. These demands create resentments, discord and unhappiness in the family. Because each wants to play the lead, to arrange the family that they want; they try to take from the family rather than give.
3. First, wife, child, entire, Each.
4. The family may become unhappy.
5. True.
6. By our willingness to face and rectify errors and convert them into assets. The alcoholic's past thus becomes the principal asset of the family and frequently it is almost the only one.
7. We place the past in God's hands and then use it to help avert death and misery for others.
   True.
8. If we believe some good and useful purpose will be served.
9. Our talk should be tempered by a spirit of love and tolerance.
10. Experiences, own.
11. True.
12. Rule, two, feet, talks, thinks, dangerous.
13. Material, spiritual, never, home, far, unselfishness, love.
14. Giving, rather than getting.
15. Religious.
16. Cooperates, values, lopsided, include, phase, disappear.
17. God would like us to keep our heads in the clouds with Him, but that our feet ought to be firmly planted on earth. That is where our fellow travelers are, and that is where our work must be done.
18. Principles, approve, practicing, adopts.
19. Beginning, face, yield, balanced.
20. No.
21. Glum, newcomers, joy, fun, cynicism, shoulders, aid, disposal, entire, overcome.
22. We have recovered, and have been given the power to help others.
23. A. Happy.
    B. Joyous.
    C. Free.
24. No.
25. Agree or Disagree.
26. True.
27. A. First Things First.
    B. Live and Let Live.
    C. Easy Does It.

Chapter 10   TO EMPLOYERS
1. True.
2. Help, disregard, drinking, lack.
3. Annoyance, weak, stupid, irresponsible.
4. Yes.
   The effect of alcohol on the brain or the mental obsession.

5.   Honesty, incredible, terrible, temporary.
6.   Discharge that person.
7.   A. You may have an employee who wants to stop drinking and wants your
         help. Maybe they are experiencing poor job performance because of their
         drinking. If so, state that you know about their drinking and you appreciate
         their abilities. With a firm attitude, advise them that you want to keep them
         but the drinking must stop.
     B. Tell them you do not intend to lecture. Express a lack of hard feelings and
         explain the nature of alcoholism as an illness.
     C. Say you believe they are gravely ill. Ask if they want to get well. Will they
         take every necessary step, submit to anything to get well, to stop drinking
         forever? If they say yes, do they really mean it, or down inside do they
         think they're fooling you and in time can have a few drinks. They should be
         thoroughly probed on these points. Be satisfied they are not deceiving
         themselves or you.
     D. You might mention the book, ALCOHOLIC ANONYMOUS, but if they think
         they can drink even a little, they might as well be discharged after the next
         bender. Either you are dealing with a person who can and will get well or
         you are not.
     E. After satisfying yourself that they want to recover and that they will go to any
         extreme to do so, you may suggest a definite course of action. The matter of
         physical treatment should, of course, be referred to a physician. You might
         help out with the cost, but the employees need to know they are fully
         responsible.
     F. Point out that the physical treatment is but a small part of the picture. They
         should understand that they must undergo a change of heart. To get over
         drinking will require a transformation of thought and attitude. The employer
         must be ready to keep this strictly a personal matter, that their alcoholic
         derelictions, the treatment about to be undertaken, will never be discussed
         without their consent.
     G. You might draw the book to the attention of the doctor who is to attend your
         employees during treatment. If the book is read the moment the patients
         are able, while acutely depressed, realization of their condition may come
         to them. Do not tell them they must abide by its suggestions; you are betting
         that the book, ALCOHOLIC ANONYMOUS, and your help will turn the trick.
     H. On their return to work, talk with them. Ask them if they think they have the
         answer. Tell them they are free to discuss their problems with you. If they
         know you understand and want to help, they will probably be off to a fast
         start. Remember, the greatest enemies for alcoholics are resentment,
         jealousy, envy, frustration, and fear. There may be times when they help
         other alcoholics during business hours. Some latitude will be helpful
         because this work is necessary to maintain their sobriety.
     I. Recovering alcoholics need to be responsible for the past and present
         and no special privileges will be required or asked for. If a relapse occurs,
         you may have to let them go. If you are sure they do not mean business,
         there is no doubt you should discharge them. If you are sure they are doing
         their utmost, you may wish to give them another chance.

J. You may want to provide a copy of ALCOHOLIC ANONYMOUS to some key employees. These people are in difficult positions. They may have friends who are employees and are experiencing trouble with alcohol. They can be a service to the business and the employee by not covering for an impaired employee. They can be an important link in getting them the help they need. People should <u>not</u> be fired just because they are alcoholic. If they want to stop, they should be afforded a real chance. If they cannot or do not want to stop, they should be discharged.

8. The same amount everyone else receives.
9. No.
10. Yes.

Chapter 11   A VISION FOR YOU

1. An insistent yearning to enjoy life as we once did and a heartbreaking obsession that some new miracle of control would enable us to do it. There was always one more attempt–and one more failure.
2. King Alcohol.
   They inhabit a mad realm of loneliness which thickens and grows blacker.
3. A. Terror.
   B. Bewilderment.
   C. Frustration.
   D. Despair.
4. The old game of drinking.
5. The alcoholic will be unable to imagine life either with alcohol or without it.
6. A. A fellowship in Alcoholics Anonymous.
   B. There you will find release from care, boredom and worry.
   C. Your imagination will be fired.
   D. Life will mean something at last.
   E. The most satisfactory years of your existence lie ahead.
   F. You will find the fellowship.
   G. Among them you will make lifelong friends.
   H. You will be bound to them with new and wonderful ties.
   I. You will escape disaster together.
   J. You will commence shoulder to shoulder your common journey.
   K. Then you will know what it means to give of yourself that others may survive and rediscover life.
   L. You will learn the full meaning of "Love thy neighbor as thyself."
7. A. That defeated drinkers will follow the suggestions in the book.
   B. That fellowships of Alcoholics Anonymous will spring up in every city and town.
8. Of course he couldn't drink but why not sit hopefully at a table, a bottle of ginger ale before him? After all, had he not been sober six months now? Perhaps he could handle, say, three drinks-no more! Fear gripped him. He was on thin ice. Again it was the old, insidious insanity–that first drink.
9. A Spiritual Experience.
10. Face their problems squarely.
11. By working directly with alcoholics. Helping them before they sober up and after they join the program.
12. It deteriorates the body and warps the mind.

13. A. Alcoholics must give their life to the <u>care</u> and <u>direction</u> of their Creator.
    B. They must be willing to do what is necessary for a Spiritual Experience.
    By working for and maintaining the Twelve Steps of A.A.
14. Must, sober, transcended, others, hours, willing, visit, failures, family.
15. A. A place where anyone interested in a spiritual way of life can meet.
    B. To provide a time and place where new people might bring their problems.
16. Yes.
17. Your loving and All Powerful Creator.
18. They are restored and united under one God, with hearts and minds attuned to the welfare of others.
19. Our, Understanding, willing, spiritual basis, help.
20. You can tap a source of power much greater than yourself if you are willing, patient and work for it.
21. A. Discovering the joy of helping others face life again.
    B. He will show you how to create the fellowship you crave.
    C. God will constantly disclose more to you and to us.
    D. When your relationship is right with Him (God), great events will come to pass for you and countless others.
    E. We shall be with you in the Fellowship of the Spirit, and you will surely meet some of us as you trudge the Road of Happy Destiny.
22. When your relationship is right with Him (God), great events will come to pass for you and countless others.
23. Agree or Disagree.
24. Agree or Disagree.

PERSONAL STORIES   DOCTOR BOB'S NIGHTMARE

1. Being an only child may have helped cause his selfishness.
2. In college.
3. Because of his enormous capacity for beer.
4. Drinking impaired his studies.
   Remain absolutely dry.
5. He was kept so busy working that he hardly left the hospital.
6. Two, stomach, drinks, excessive.
7. Three, hospital, smuggle, quart, steal, alcohol.
8. A morning drink meant Bob would be unfit for work and unable to earn money to buy more alcohol; therefore he used drugs to quiet the morning jitters.
9. Seventeen years.
10. He had developed alcoholism. The mental obsession (mental) to drink made it impossible to quit entirely and the phenomenon of craving (physical) made controlling the amount impossible.
11. Something of a spiritual nature that Bob did not have.
    His wife.
12. Alcoholism, experienced, spiritual.
    True.
13. Relieved.
    True.

14. A. Sense of duty.
    B. It is a pleasure.
    C. Because in so doing he was paying his debt to the man who took time to pass what he had learned to Bob.
    D. Because every time he did it he took out a little more insurance for himself against a possible slip.

15. A. Atheism.
    B. Agnosticism.
    C. Skepticism.

16. A. But if you really and truly want to quit drinking liquor for good and all, and sincerely feel that you must have some help, we know that we have the answer for you. It never fails, if you go about it with one half the zeal you have been in the habit of showing when you were getting another drink. (emphasis added.)
    B. Your Heavenly Father will never let you down!

17. Agree or Disagree.

18. Agree or Disagree.

References

ALCOHOLICS ANONYMOUS. 3rd ed.
New York: A.A. World Services, Inc., 1990.
TWELVE STEPS AND TWELVE TRADITIONS.
New York: A.A. World Services, Inc., 1990.

Suggested Readings

ALCOHOLICS ANONYMOUS COMES OF AGE.
New York: A.A. World Services, Inc., 1983.
AS BILL SEES IT.
New York: A.A. World Services, Inc., 1979.
BEST OF THE GRAPEVINE.
New York: The AA Grapevine, Inc., 1985.
Blauner Robert. ALIENATION AND FREEDOM.
Chicago: The University of Chicago Press, 1964.
Bloodworth, Venice. KEY TO YOURSELF.
Marina del Rey, CA.: DeVorss & Company, 1952 & 1980.
Buscaglia, Leo. LIVING, LOVING & LEARNING.
New York: Ballantine Books, 1982.
Buscaglia, Leo. LOVING EACH OTHER.
New York: Holt, Rinehart and Winston, 1984.
Buscaglia, Leo. PERSONHOOD.
New York: Ballantine Books, 1978.
Buscaglia, Leo. THE FALL OF FREDDY THE LEAF.
New York: Holt, Rinehart and Winston, 1982.
Cole-Whittaker, Terry. WHAT YOU THINK OF ME IS NONE OF MY BUSINESS.
LaJolla, CA.: Oak Tree Publications, Inc., 1979.
Coser, Lewis. THE PLEASURES OF SOCIOLOGY.
New York: Mentor Book, 1980.
Dember, William, Jenkins, James and Teyler, Timothy. GENERAL PSYCHOLOGY.
Hillsdale, NJ.: Lawrence Erlbaum Associates, Publishers, 1984.
DR. BOB AND THE GOOD OLDTIMERS.
New York: A.A. World Services, Inc., 1980.
Ford, Edward. CHOOSING TO LOVE.
San Francisco: Harper & Row, 1983.
Ford, Edward. FREEDOM FROM STRESS.
Scottsdale, AZ.: Brandt Publishing, 1989.
Ford, Edward. LOVE GUARANTEED.
San Francisco: Harper & Row, 1987.
Ford, Edward. PERMANENT LOVE.
Minneapolis: Winston Press, Inc., 1979.
Ford, Edward. WHY MARRIAGE.
Niles, IL.: Argus Communications, 1974.
Glasser, William. CONTROL THEORY.
New York: Harper & Row, 1984.
Glasser, William. POSITIVE ADDICTION.
New York: Harper & Row, 1976.
Glasser, William. REALITY THERAPY.
New York: Harper & Row, 1965.

Suggested Readings

Hershey, Terry. INTIMACY: WHERE DO I GO TO FIND LOVE.
  Laguna Hills, CA.: Merit Books, 1984.
HOLY BIBLE. THE NEW KING JAMES VERSION.
  New York: Thomas Nelson Publishers, 1983.
James, William. THE PRINCIPLES OF PSYCHOLOGY.
  Cambridge, MA.: Harvard University Press, 1983.
James, William. THE VARIETIES OF RELIGIOUS EXPERIENCE.
  New York: Penguin Books, 1982.
Jampolsky, Gerald. TEACH ONLY LOVE.
  New York: Bantam Books, 1983.
Johnson, Robert. WE: UNDERSTAND THE PSYCHOLOGY OF ROMANTIC LOVE.
  San Francisco: Harper & Row 1983.
Jung, Carl. ANALYTICAL PSYCHOLOGY: ITS THEORY AND PRACTICE.
  New York: Vintage Books, 1968.
Jung, Carl. PSYCHOLOGICAL TYPES.
  Princeton, NJ.: Princeton University Press, 1971.
Jung, Carl. PSYCHOLOGY & RELIGION.
  Binghamton, NY.: Vail-Ballou Press, Inc., 1938.
Kurtz, Ernest. NOT–GOD.
  Center City, MN.: Hazelden, 1979.
Lawrence, Brother. THE PRACTICE OF THE PRESENCE OF GOD.
  Mount Vernon, NY.: Peter Pauper Press, 1963.
LeShan, Lawrence. HOW TO MEDITATE.
  New York: Bantam Book, 1974.
Mandino, Og. MISSION SUCCESS!
  New York: Bantam Books, 1986.
Mandino, Og. THE GREATEST MIRACLE IN THE WORLD.
  New York: Bantam Books, 1975.
Mandino, Og. THE GREATEST SALESMAN IN THE WORLD.
  New York: Bantam Books, 1968.
Mandino, Og. THE GREATEST SECRET IN THE WORLD.
  New York: Bantam Books, 1972.
Mandino, Og. THE GREATEST SUCCESS IN THE WORLD.
  New York: Bantam Books, 1981.
PASS IT ON.
  New York: A.A. World Services, Inc., 1984.
Rodgers, Harrell, Jr. THE COST OF HUMAN NEGLECT.
  Armonk, NY.: M. E. Sharpe, Inc., 1982.
Russell, Bertrand. A HISTORY OF WESTERN PHILOSOPHY.
  New York: Simon and Schuster, 1964.
THE A.A. SERVICE MANUAL.
  New York: A.A. World Services, Inc., 1989.
THE LANGUAGE OF THE HEART: BILL W.'s GRAPEVINE WRITINGS.
  New York: The AA Grapevine, Inc., 1988.
Wubbolding, Robert. USING REALITY THERAPY.
  New York: Harper & Row, 1988.
Zeitlin, Irving. THE SOCIAL CONDITION OF HUMANITY.
  Oxford, NY.: Oxford University Press, 1984.

- - - - - - - - - - - - - - - -

MAIL TO ▶ **GLAD PUBLICATION** • <u>MONEY ORDER ONLY</u> • <u>NO CHECKS</u> ◀ MAIL TO
966 PALMWOOD DRIVE • SPARKS, NV 89434 • 702-356-7856

Ordered By: PLEASE PRINT
Call for volume discount rate

Name

Address

City   State   Zip

PHONE (In case we have questions about your order)
(_____) – _____ – _____

ALLOW 4 to 6 WEEKS FOR DELIVERY
* NEVADA RESIDENTS ONLY
MONEY ORDER ONLY – NO CHECKS
BOOK SHIPPING WEIGHT 1.75 lbs.
CALL FOR VOLUME DISCOUNT RATE

Ship To: PLEASE PRINT

Name

Address

City   State   Zip

NUMBER OF BOOKS ORDERED X $16.00 _____

Trudging the Road
A Work /Study
Journey through the Twelve Steps
of Alcoholics Anonymous
ISBN 0-9629091-0-6

SALES TAX *

SHIPPING

TOTAL $

Shipping, Handling, Postage; U.S. Only: 1-2 lbs. $4.00, 3-6 lbs. $6.00, 7-9 lbs. $8.00, 10-13 lbs. $10.00,
14-16 lbs. $12.00, 17-18 lbs. $13.00, 20 lbs. & over $15.00 + $0.50 for each additional pound over 20 lbs.

- - - - - - - - - - - - - - - -

MAIL TO ▶ **GLAD PUBLICATION** • <u>MONEY ORDER ONLY</u> • <u>NO CHECKS</u> ◀ MAIL TO
966 PALMWOOD DRIVE • SPARKS, NV 89434 • 702-356-7856

Ordered By: PLEASE PRINT
Call for volume discount rate

Name

Address

City   State   Zip

PHONE (In case we have questions about your order)
(_____) – _____ – _____

ALLOW 4 to 6 WEEKS FOR DELIVERY
* NEVADA RESIDENTS ONLY
MONEY ORDER ONLY – NO CHECKS
BOOK SHIPPING WEIGHT 1.75 lbs.
CALL FOR VOLUME DISCOUNT RATE

Ship To: PLEASE PRINT

Name

Address

City   State   Zip

NUMBER OF BOOKS ORDERED X $16.00 _____

Trudging the Road
A Work /Study
Journey through the Twelve Steps
of Alcoholics Anonymous
ISBN 0-9629091-0-6

SALES TAX *

SHIPPING

TOTAL $

Shipping, Handling, Postage; U.S. Only: 1-2 lbs. $4.00, 3-6 lbs. $6.00, 7-9 lbs. $8.00, 10-13 lbs. $10.00,
14-16 lbs. $12.00, 17-18 lbs. $13.00, 20 lbs. & over $15.00 + $0.50 for each additional pound over 20 lbs.